THE
IMMIGRANT
COOKBOOK

THE IMMIGRANT COOKBOOK

Recipes that Make America Great

COLLECTED AND EDITED
BY LEYLA MOUSHABECK

Interlink Books

An imprint of Interlink Publishing Group, Inc.
Northampton, Massachusetts

For my mother, Ruth, the first
immigrant to inspire my love of food

—LM

First published in 2018 by

INTERLINK BOOKS
An imprint of Interlink Publishing Group, Inc.
46 Crosby Street, Northampton, Massachusetts 01060
www.interlinkbooks.com

Library of Congress Cataloging-in-Publication Data available

ISBN 978-1-56656-038-2 (hardback)

General Editor: Michel S. Moushabeck
Commissioning Editor: Leyla Moushabeck
Photography: Ricarius Photography, unless otherwise noted (see page 215)
Design and Art Direction: Julian D. Ramirez
Proofreaders: Jennifer M. Staltare, Whitney Sanderson

Printed and bound in Korea

10 9 8 7 6 5 4 3 2 1

I believe in you, and I believe in your destiny.

I believe that you are contributors to this new civilization.

I believe that you have inherited from your forefathers an ancient dream, a song, a prophecy, which you can proudly lay as a gift of gratitude upon the lap of America.

I believe that you can say to the founders of this great nation, "Here I am, a youth, a young tree whose roots were plucked from the hills of Lebanon, yet I am deeply rooted here, and I would be fruitful."

—Excerpted from *To Young Americans of Syrian Origin* by Kahlil Gibran

CONTENTS

INTRODUCTION

When I returned home to the US after living and studying abroad for over a decade, I was struck by the powerful bonds between identity and cultural heritage felt by so many Americans. More than almost anywhere else in the world, we are a land of immigrants. At this time, over 42 million people living in the United States have come here from other countries. As with past generations, many have come seeking refuge from political or economic turmoil; others, simply looking for opportunity for themselves, their children and loved ones. But whatever our families' origins, journeys here or relationships to this country's history, our identity as Americans is intimately linked to our ties to our native lands.

For many of us, this identity is best summed up in the kitchen, by the foods we ate as children, lovingly prepared as special treats or for comfort, bringing families and communities together, and maintaining ties to heritage and homelands. My own kitchen is peppered with the flavors of my British and Palestinian upbringing, learned via phone calls talking me through steps and spices, or taking notes while my mother or aunts added a bit of cumin, or a pinch of allspice. Along the way, I have picked up the traditional Colombian dishes of my family-by-marriage, and tried my hand at dishes from the many cultures encountered in the Brooklyn neighborhood where I was born. It thrills me that I am building my own small culinary legacy. My one-year-old son, newly discovering the delights of solid foods, is already guaranteed to eat anything we slather in hummus.

Newly arrived immigrants, bringing ingredients and cooking techniques from their home countries, continue to influence how Americans cook and eat. Almost all of the foods we think of as American specialties can be traced to immigrants, who brought or adapted them: pizza, bagels, pretzels, apple pie, waffles, hot dogs, tacos, hamburgers and the ice cream cone all originate with immigrants—from Europe, Latin America, Africa, Asia or the Middle East. Absorbed into the mainstream, they have been popularized around the world as American exports. I once found myself in a Brooklyn-themed restaurant in Bogota and ate Mexican-style grilled corn. And as ingredients and information become increasingly available, we gain more access to the cuisines of immigrant America. New generations take for granted the wealth of internationally sourced ingredients available in our grocery stores, and the interaction of cultures can inspire new kinds of food.

Bon Appétit's March 2017 issue was dedicated to the children of immigrants, after editors noticed that so many of their top restaurant choices in the country were run by the chefs "transforming the cuisines they grew up eating into something undeniably modern and uniquely American." *Bon Appétit* editor-in-chief Adam Rapoport summed it up in his interview with the *Washingtonian*:

> America's food is not all about tradition and tried-and-true recipes. It's about this constant influx of new flavors coming into this country, and both appreciating those flavors and dishes, and finding a way to reinvent them and riff on them in an American way.

In these troubling times of anti-immigrant rhetoric, making life difficult for many who have sought a new home in the US, there is also a growing movement to acknowledge these groups for the cultural wealth and heritage they bring to this country, including their culinary traditions. In *The Immigrant Cookbook*, you will find some of the people, experiences and foods that make up America's multifaceted culinary landscape.

In a practical sense, immigrants also play an integral role in the business of food, making up the vast majority of the lowest paying labor in America's farms, food-production factories, grocery stores, and restaurants. Almost 80 percent of US farm laborers are foreign-born, according to a National Agricultural Workers Survey, and the restaurant industry is the largest private-sector employer of all immigrants to the US, many without the legal protection of official documentation (ROC United). The restaurant industry's dependence on immigrants was exemplified during the protest "A Day without Immigrants," of which contributor to this cookbook José Andrés was a prominent spokesperson, shutting down businesses nationwide early in 2017. Ignoring the rights and needs of this group has ramifications extending far beyond the recipes we cook, the delis we frequent, or the restaurants where we eat.

But political divisiveness and mistrust have turned many to food as a medium for collaboration—serving their communities, inspiring connection, compassion, understanding, and activism. Contributor Tunde Wey's traveling dinner series, for example, challenges diners to active discussion about race and the issues facing Black Americans; Dalia Mortada documents the stories of Syrians now in the Diaspora as part of her project, *Savoring Syria*; and Claus Meyer's latest restaurant, The Brownsville Community Culinary Center, in Brooklyn, brings culinary resources and training to the Brownsville neighborhood. Each of the contributors in this book is an ambassador of their cuisine, creating awareness and understanding of their culture through food.

In reading their stories and sharing their food, you are connecting with that culture—inviting a piece of it into your home, to sustain you and your family, giving you a small glimpse into another place and experience. Every dish in this book will transport you somewhere—perhaps somewhere new to you, but all are on your doorstep. They are festive dishes, or everyday comfort food. They are dishes served after synagogue, or for Christmas dinner, or to break the Ramadan fast. Some are traditional recipes, passed down through generations; some are a rediscovery of cultures temporarily forgotten. Whether the dish is traditional, contemporary or the result of cultural collision, each holds emotional significance to the chef who created it, drawing on childhood memories, experiences and their unique relationship to their chosen home. With each bite, you can taste a distinct element of warmth, like a hug from your mother, or returning home after a journey. As a collection, *The Immigrant Cookbook* reflects not only a celebration of diverse culinary traditions, but it captures the spirit of what makes America great.

—Leyla Moushabeck
Brooklyn, New York

APPETIZERS

Enrique Olvera   ORIGIN: MEXICO

SCALLOP AGUACHILE

Food is a powerful method of communication and we experience culture through it. Immigration and globalized exchange are leading us to blur borders and get to know and understand each other's forms of living and cooking, embracing and mixing different ingredients, techniques, and flavors. This is my approach to food. The idea is first and foremost to eat well, and the matter of where the dish comes from becomes less and less important. This dish is about building bridges between a Japanese *yuzu-kosho* and Mexican *aguachile* by replacing the chilies with wasabi, and giving equal value to the jicama and the scallops. If possible, look for fresh wasabi root, available in Asian grocery stores.

Juice the cucumbers in a juicer to make 1½ cups (350 ml) juice. Alternatively, blend or process the cucumbers to a fine pulp and strain through a chinois sieve or cheesecloth into a bowl. Set aside.

If using, make the cilantro oil: Prepare a small bowl of ice water. Bring a small pot of water to a boil. Blanch the cilantro leaves in the boiling water, and quickly transfer to the ice water. Carefully squeeze out all the water and spread the cilantro out on paper towels to dry. Combine the blanched cilantro and oil in a small blender and process until smooth. Strain through a chinois sieve or cheesecloth into a bowl.

In a large stockpot over medium heat, dissolve the salt in 5 cups (1.2 liters) water and allow to cool. Soak the scallop slices in the cooled saltwater for ten minutes, then rinse under cold running water and drain, patting them dry with paper towels. Set aside in the refrigerator.

Prepare a bowl of ice water. Half-fill a medium pot with water, season with salt, and bring to a boil. Add the jicama slices and boil just until al dente, then drain and transfer to the ice water. Line a tray with paper towels. Drain the jicama slices, arrange them on the tray, and set aside in the refrigerator.

In a mixing bowl, combine the vinaigrette ingredients and mix well. Season with salt, to taste.

Arrange the scallop and jicama slices in individual bowls. Spoon about 4 tablespoons of the vinaigrette into each bowl, and garnish as desired (pictured at this step). Just before serving, pour in just enough cucumber juice to almost submerge the slices in liquid. Sprinkle a few drops of cilantro oil over each dish, and serve immediately.

Enrique Olvera is a leader of Mexico's new gastronomy, fueled by a constant exploration of Mexico's ingredients and culinary history. In 2000, at the age of 24, he opened the globally-recognized restaurant, Pujol, in Mexico City. He now also owns four outposts of Eno in Mexico City; Manta, in Los Cabos; and Cosme and Atla in New York City. He is author of *Mexico from the Inside Out*. Over time, he has created a cosmopolitan cuisine that is modern in approach but anchored by Mexican tradition. He prefers not to categorize his dishes. Instead, it is flavor that drives and guides him. He divides his time between New York and Mexico City.

Serves 4 to 6

1 lb 5 oz (600 g) cucumbers (about 2 English), trimmed
1 cup (10½ oz/300 g) salt, plus more to season
8 very large dry-packed scallops (about 8 oz/225 g), side muscle removed, very thinly sliced
1 jicama, peeled and very thinly sliced into disks

CILANTRO OIL

6 cilantro sprigs, leaves picked
3 tablespoons grapeseed oil

VINAIGRETTE

1 Persian cucumber, finely diced
½ bunch cilantro, finely chopped
2 tablespoons finely chopped wasabi root, or 1½ tablespoons wasabi paste
2 tablespoons finely chopped ginger
1½ tablespoons finely chopped white onion
½ cup (120 ml) extra virgin olive oil
3 serrano chilies, finely chopped
Juice of 4 limes

GARNISHES

½ small red onion, finely chopped
1–2 serrano chili peppers, sliced
Delfino cilantro sprigs or cilantro leaves (optional)

Jesus Delgado ORIGIN: PERU
TIRADITO LIMA BANGKOK

I grew up in Lima, Peru, where my family owned and operated a small market. My childhood was spent in the kitchen, watching my grandfather, who was an incredible cook. As a chef, I have always been drawn to working with seafood, especially in Peruvian ceviche and *tiradito* dishes. *Tiradito* is a dish of raw or lightly seared fish cut in a style similar to sashimi, and topped with a piquant citrus dressing and a selection of textural garnishes. This recipe perfectly embodies Peru's multicultural cuisine, with influences from Japan and Thailand. It's bright, beautiful and, most importantly, delicious.

Preheat a grill or griddle pan until screaming hot and prepare a bowl of ice water. Sear the tuna fillets for about 30 seconds on each side, then transfer immediately to the ice water. Set aside for 2 to 3 minutes, then drain and pat dry.

Arrange the watermelon radish slices in the bottom of a wide, shallow serving bowl, creating a base for the tuna.

Cut the tuna into slices around 1 inch by 1 inch by 1½ inches (2 cm by 2 cm by 4 cm). Arrange over the radishes.

In a separate bowl, mix the chopped onion, lime juice, panca paste, honey, soy sauce, tamarind, coconut milk, and a pinch of salt. Pour the mixture over the tuna.

Scatter with the mango, peanuts, scallions, and chopped cilantro. Garnish with the cilantro sprigs or leaves, jalapeño slices, cucumber pieces, and cherry peppers, and serve immediately.

Jesus Delgado is executive chef of Tanta in Chicago, a collaboration with well-known South American Chef Gastón Acurio. Jesus was born and raised in Peru, one of the world's most diverse and eclectic food cultures. He worked at number of Chinese- and Japanese-influenced restaurants in Lima, before landing at Acurio's La Mar Cebicheria in 2007 as a line cook. By 2011, Jesus had worked his way up and excelled in the role of ceviche chef, creating a diverse menu of traditional and unexpected fresh fish dishes and other cold plates, cementing his reputation for showcasing Peruvian seafood in distinctive and unexpected ways. He moved to Chicago, Illinois in 2013 to lead Tanta's kitchen.

Serves 4

14 oz (400 g) tuna fillets
3 large watermelon radishes, cut into thin strips
1 small or ½ large red onion, finely diced
Scant 2 cups (440 ml) freshly squeezed lime juice (about 10 limes)
1½ teaspoons aji panca paste
1 teaspoon honey
1 teaspoon soy sauce
1 tablespoon tamarind paste
2 tablespoons coconut milk
Salt
3 tablespoons finely diced mango
1 tablespoon chopped peanuts
½ teaspoon chopped scallions
½ teaspoon chopped cilantro

GARNISHES
Micro cilantro sprigs or regular cilantro leaves
Thinly sliced jalapeño peppers
Cucumber slices, quartered
Sweet cherry peppers

Emma Bengtsson ORIGIN: SWEDEN

RYE PANCAKES WITH PORK BELLY AND LINGONBERRIES

I grew up eating these pancakes at home in Falkenberg, Sweden. What I love most about them is that the rye flour creates a great balance between sweet, salty, and acidic flavors; meaning, they can be served as a sweet or savory course. When I made them as a kid, I would often save leftovers to eat with vanilla ice cream and berry compote, while at Aquavit we serve them with bacon, as a savory amuse-bouche. Look for fresh or frozen lingonberries in specialty grocery stores, or substitute cranberries or red currants. You will need to chill the batter and the berries in advance, so plan accordingly.

First, prepare the lingonberries: Combine the sugar and vinegar in a bowl or jug. Place the berries in a jar or plastic tub and pour the vinegar mixture over them. Cover and chill overnight.

Next, make the pancake batter: In a large bowl, combine the eggs and sugar. In a separate bowl, combine the rye and all-purpose flours. Gradually stir half the flour into the egg mixture, making sure that no lumps have formed. Mix in the cream, then gradually add the rest of the flour, mixing until the batter is smooth. Finally, mix in the milk and salt. Cover and chill the batter overnight, or for at least 4 hours.

In a mixing bowl, whisk the mustard and crème fraîche to soft peaks. Cover and chill until you are ready to serve.

Half an hour before you would like to serve, preheat the oven to 325°F (160°C) and line a baking sheet with parchment paper. Arrange the bacon slices on the pan and bake until crisp, 10 to 20 minutes.

Meanwhile, make the pancakes: Heat an 8 inch (20 cm) frying pan over medium heat. Very lightly grease the pan with melted butter. Pour in about 3 tablespoons of the batter, or just enough to cover the base of the pan in a thin layer, about twice the thickness of a crêpe. Cook for 1 to 2 minutes, until the batter is set, then flip the pancake, and cook for an additional 1 to 2 minutes. Repeat, adding more butter as necessary, until you have used all the batter (you should have about 12 pancakes).

Chop the bacon strips. Fold the pancakes into quarters, and divide between four plates. Sprinkle with the bacon and lingonberries. Dollop with the mustard crème fraîche, and garnish with fresh thyme leaves.

Serves 4

3 tablespoons whole-grain mustard
1 cup (7 oz/200 g) crème fraîche
14 oz (400 g) thick-cut bacon
    (sliced slab bacon is best)
About 7 tablespoons (3½ oz/100 g)
    unsalted butter
8 thyme sprigs, leaves stripped

PRESERVED LINGONBERRIES

¾ cup (3 oz/85 g) lingonberries (fresh or
    frozen), red currants, or cranberries
1½ tablespoons sugar
1½ tablespoons distilled white vinegar

PANCAKES

4 eggs
Generous ¼ cup (2 oz/60 g) sugar
Generous ½ cup (2 oz/60g) light,
    medium, or dark rye flour
1¼ cups (5½ oz/150 g) all-purpose flour
1 cup (240 ml) heavy cream
1¼ cups (300 ml) whole milk
2 teaspoons salt

Emma Bengtsson grew up in Falkenberg, Sweden, and became interested in the culinary arts at a young age, thanks to her grandmother. Emma trained at Stockholm's Hotel and Restaurant School and went on to work at Edsbacka Krog, where she discovered her love of pastry. After working in some of Sweden's top kitchens, including Restaurant Prinsen and Operakällaren, Emma joined Aquavit in 2010 as pastry chef. In Spring 2014, she became executive chef, garnering a second Michelin star for Aquavit, making her the second female chef in the US to run a two-star kitchen, and the first ever Swedish female chef to do so. She lives in New York.

Reem Assil ORIGIN: SYRIA, PALESTINE

REEM'S MUHAMMARA

Muhammara is my homecoming. I discovered this addicting dip as an adult and fell in love with it when I went back to Syria in 2010. At the time, I was soul-searching in my father's homeland and started to open my eyes to all the richness of my Syrian identity, particularly through the food and hospitality. Up until then I was only exposed to my mother's Lebanese and Palestinian cooking and wasn't as well-versed in Syrian food. In every home in Syria, my family would serve multiple mezze dips with dinner and *muhammara* was always a centerpiece. It has the perfect combination of tangy, nutty, and spicy flavors. And it looks beautiful on a dinner spread. I began to feature it at my farmers' markets and catering, and it became an instant hit. Now it is a staple in my restaurant and represents my Syrian pride. Look for Aleppo pepper and pomegranate molasses in Middle Eastern or specialty grocery stores, and you can easily halve or double this recipe to suit your needs. Serve with your favorite bread.

Preheat your oven to 400°F (200°C). Line a baking sheet with parchment paper and place the peppers on it. Roast until the skins are charred, about 30 minutes, turning them over once or twice. Transfer to a sealable bag, or a bowl covered with plastic wrap, and set aside until cool enough to handle. Tear them open, remove the stem and seeds, and peel the skins.

   Working in batches, if necessary, combine the walnuts and breadcrumbs in a food processor, and process to a cornmeal-like texture. Add the roasted peppers, pomegranate molasses, lemon juice, garlic, cumin, Aleppo pepper, and salt, and pulse until smooth, turning off the machine and scraping down the sides of the bowl from time to time.

   With the processor running, slowly add the olive oil, and blend until the oil is completely incorporated. Taste and add salt, if needed.

   Garnish as desired and serve chilled or at room temperature.

Makes 4 cups (2 lb/1 kg)

2½ lb (1.2 kg) red bell peppers (7 large)
2½ cups (9 oz/250 g) walnut halves
1 cup (2 oz/60 g) panko breadcrumbs
2 tablespoons pomegranate molasses
1 tablespoon lemon juice
3–4 garlic cloves
1 teaspoon cumin
1 tablespoon Aleppo pepper flakes
1 teaspoon salt
⅓ cup (75 ml) extra virgin olive oil
Pomegranate seeds, walnuts, or
   chopped parsley, to garnish (optional)

Reem Assil is the chef and founder of Reem's in Oakland, California. Reem's was founded with a passion for the flavors of Arab street-corner bakeries and the vibrant communities where they're located. Growing up in a Palestinian-Syrian household, Reem was surrounded by the aromas and tastes of food from her homeland and the connections they evoked of her heritage, family, and community. Before dedicating herself to a culinary career, Reem worked for a decade as a community and labor organizer, and brings the warmth of community to all her events. In 2017, she graduated from La Cocina, a competitive food business incubator program focusing on immigrant women.

Hanif Sadr ORIGIN: IRAN

SMOKY EGGPLANT DIP WITH POMEGRANATES AND WALNUTS

Kaleh Kabob

Kaleh kabob is a dish from the Caspian region of Gilan province, where I spent summers as a child on my grandparents' farm. The Berkeley hills remind me so much of this region and its plants, flowers, and citrus groves. The recipe showcases two important ingredients in northern Iranian cuisine: walnuts and pomegranates, which both originated in Iran. It's full of smoky charred eggplant, pomegranate juice, and basil, mixed with garlic and mint. It has a lovely mild purple color and makes a fantastic dip or a very light meal, served with crackers, flatbread, or *kateh* (northern Iranian soft-cooked rice). Look for pomegranate molasses in Middle Eastern or specialty stores, or you can substitute tamarind paste, if you can't find it.

Cook the eggplants over an open flame on your grill or stovetop, or in the oven: To cook on the stove, line your burners with foil to protect them. Place the eggplants directly on the flames, and roast, turning frequently, until the skin is charred all over and the flesh is soft, 15 to 20 minutes. To oven-roast, preheat your oven to 400°F (200°C) and place the eggplants on a baking tray. Roast until the skin is charred and the insides are soft, about 45 minutes.

Remove the skin, finely chop the flesh, and transfer to a colander to drain for at least 20 minutes. Season the chopped eggplant with the salt and black pepper and set aside.

Place the walnuts in a food processor and pulse until finely ground.

In a large mixing bowl, combine the eggplants, ground walnuts, pomegranate juice and molasses, basil, mint, garlic, and olive oil, and mix well. Taste and adjust the seasoning, if desired. Set aside for 30 minutes, or up to 24 hours.

When you are ready to serve, give it good stir, and garnish as desired with the pomegranate seeds and basil leaves.

Makes 6 cups (3 lb/1.4 kg)

5 lb (2.25 kg) eggplants (4 to 5)
¼ teaspoon salt, plus more to taste
¼ teaspoon ground black pepper, plus more to taste
1 cup (4 oz/115 g) chopped walnuts
1 cup (240 ml) pomegranate juice
1 tablespoon pomegranate molasses
1 cup (1½ oz/40 g) finely chopped basil, plus a few whole leaves, to garnish
2 tablespoons finely sliced mint
1-2 garlic cloves, minced
½ teaspoon extra virgin olive oil
¼ cup (1½ oz/40 g) pomegranate seeds, to garnish (optional)

Hanif Sadr was born in Paris, France, and raised in Tehran, Iran. He is chef and co-founder of Komaaj, a Northern Iranian pop-up restaurant and catering company based in Berkeley, California.

Laila El-Haddad ORIGIN: PALESTINE

GAZAN HOT TOMATO AND DILL SALAD
Dagga (Salata Ghazawiyya)

This is the most frequently served salad in Gaza, with a hot bite that makes it a fantastic accompaniment to meaty stews or rice dishes. *Dagga*, which is a variation of the word meaning "pounded" in Arabic, is commonly scooped up with Arabic bread, and has a consistency similar to that of a Mexican salsa. This dish must be made in a mortar and pestle with a rough interior (in Gaza, a *zibdiya*). Don't bother using a food processor!

Though she herself was of mixed Circassian and Kurdish-Damascene ancestry, my late maternal grandmother, il-Sitt Laila, as she was endearingly known, was fond of this classic, and used to refer to it as "the centerpiece of the Gazan table." It was probably the first recipe I learned from my mother, who often tasked us young children with the rhythmic exercise of mashing the garlic.

Dagga is one of those recipes you are likely to find Gazan Palestinians making the world over, probably in a *zibdiya* they've inherited, a great source of pride. The original mortars are extremely hard to come by due to constant closures. They are fashioned from the rich, red clay in Gaza, and a constant reminder that though we may be thousands of miles (and often an unattainable reality) away, we have a part of that earth with us, and we can taste home wherever we go.

You can substitute 1 tablespoon dill seeds for the fresh dill and 2 tablespoons finely chopped onions for the garlic. The dill seeds should be ground in the mortar thoroughly in a circular motion along with some of the salt, before adding the onions and proceeding with the recipe.

Serves 4

2 garlic cloves, peeled
½ teaspoon salt
2–3 hot green chili peppers, such as jalapeño or serrano
¼ cup (½ oz/15 g) finely chopped dill
3 ripe medium tomatoes, coarsely chopped
Juice of ½ lemon
Extra virgin olive oil
Arabic flatbread or pita, to serve

Using a large mortar and pestle, mash garlic and salt to a paste. Coarsely chop the chili peppers, removing some of the membranes if you prefer less heat. Add the peppers to the mortar and crush until tender. Stir in the dill. Using a circular motion, grind the dill until fragrant.

Add the tomatoes and pound until salad reaches a thick salsa-like consistency. Transfer to a serving dish, stir in the lemon juice, and then mix the entire salad well and even out the top with the back of a spoon. Drench the top with a rich olive oil, but don't stir it in.

Serve with Arabic flatbread on the side for scooping it up.

Laila El-Haddad is a Maryland-based freelance journalist, documentarian, and cookbook author. She is the author of *The Gaza Kitchen: A Palestinian Culinary Journey*. She frequently writes on the intersection of food and politics and she is currently working on a book about the history of Islam in America, as told through food.

SALADS

Daniel Boulud ORIGIN: FRANCE

LYONNAISE SALAD WITH LARDONS
Salade Lyonnaise aux Lardons

I've been serving this dish at Bar Boulud (in New York, London, and
Boston) since the opening—and it's always been a bestseller. To me,
the salad is just so French. It's a classic and a staple at many casual
bistros or *bouchons*, and it's just as easy to make at home. Sautéed
chicken livers and pork belly are lightly glazed with sherry vinegar and
chicken jus, then served warm over a nest of frisée, with a perfectly
poached egg. Like many of my favorite French dishes, the success is in
the simplicity. With its rich flavors and humble ingredients, this salad
takes me right back to my parents' farm outside of Lyon. You can find
chicken jus or demi-glace online at www.dartagnan.com or in specialty
grocery stores.

Whisk together the Dijon mustard, red wine vinegar, and ¼ cup (60 ml)
of the olive oil. Season with salt and pepper to taste, and set aside.

Fill a medium saucepot with lightly salted water and the white
vinegar; bring to just below a simmer. Crack the eggs, one at a time, into
the water and cook for 3 minutes; then remove with a slotted spoon.
Turn off the heat, but keep the pot of warm water for reheating the eggs.

In a large sauté pan, warm the remaining olive oil over medium
heat, add the bacon lardons, and gently render the fat for 2 to 3 minutes.
Add the bread cubes to the pan, and toast in the bacon fat until both are
golden brown, then remove the croutons, leaving some fat in the pan.

Season the chicken livers with salt and pepper, sear in the same
pan for 1 minute on each side, and then add the shallots. After another
30 seconds, add the sherry vinegar, followed by the chicken jus, cooked
bacon, and herbs. Reduce the heat to low and cook for a further 1 minute,
spooning the sauce over the bacon and livers to glaze.

Toss the frisée with the vinaigrette, and divide among 4 salad bowls.
Return the poached eggs to the warm water for a few seconds, then drain
and nestle one into the middle of each salad. Spoon the livers and bacon,
along with the sauce, over the top. Add the croutons, sprinkle the eggs
with chives, and serve.

A native of Lyon, France, **Daniel Boulud** is considered one of America's leading
culinary authorities and one of the most revered French chefs in New York, his
home since 1982. Daniel is chef-owner of 14 restaurants around the world, and
is best known for his eponymous, exquisitely refined DANIEL on Manhattan's
Upper East Side. Daniel is also the author of nine cookbooks and the recipient of
numerous awards, including the James Beard Foundation's Outstanding Chef and
Outstanding Restaurateur. He has been a generous supporter and co-president
of Citymeals-on-Wheels for more than two decades, and is chairman of the
Ment'Or BKB Foundation.

Serves 4

½ teaspoon Dijon mustard
2 tablespoons red wine vinegar
¼ cup (60 ml) plus 2 tablespoons
   good extra virgin olive oil
Salt and ground white pepper
1 tablespoon white vinegar
4 eggs
8 oz (225 g) slab bacon, cut into lardons
   (¼ inch/6 mm thick batons)
1 loaf sourdough bread, cut into
   1 inch (2 cm) cubes
2 shallots, finely minced
12 oz (350 g) chicken livers, rinsed well,
   trimmed, and patted dry
1½ tablespoons sherry vinegar
¼ cup (60 ml) chicken jus or
   demi-glace, optional
3 large heads frisée, light green
   parts only, rinsed
1 tablespoon chopped parsley
1 tablespoon chopped chives,
   plus more to serve
1 tablespoon chopped chervil

Ignacio Mattos   ORIGIN: URUGUAY, ITALY

FENNEL SALAD WITH CASTELVETRANO OLIVES AND PROVOLONE

I chose this recipe to honor my grandma's cooking and her Italian heritage. Immigrant-Italian food is what I grew up with in Uruguay. While not necessarily traditional, this salad is inspired by classic southern Italian ingredients. It reflects the spirit and drive of those who came to the US seeking better lives for themselves or their families back home. Food has always been what has brought us together.

Cut the tops and stems off the fennel bulbs. Thinly slice the stems and coarsely chop the fronds. Place the fronds and stems in a bowl with the olives. Add the oil, vinegar, red pepper flakes, and black pepper, and mix until well coated.

Using a mandolin if you have one, shave the fennel into thin slices. (You can use a vegetable peeler if you don't have a mandolin: cut the fennel into quarters and peel the cut side.) Season the fennel with the lemon zest and juice and mix.

Pile the olive mixture in the center of four serving plates and top each plate with the shaved fennel. Grate provolone cheese on top to your liking.

Ignacio Mattos is co-owner and chef of Estela, Café Altro Paradiso, and Flora Bar at the Met Breuer in New York. He was born in Uruguay and learned to cook in the kitchens of grilling master Francis Mallman and Slow Food legend Alice Waters. Per *New York Times* critic Pete Wells: "[Ignacio's] dishes are original and, in their way, simple, and it's that combination that makes you want to give in to them." In 2017, Ignacio received his third nomination for the James Beard Award for Best Chef, New York. Ignacio cooks food that is comforting and memorable, reflecting his varied experiences and the cultures of New York City, the city he now calls home.

Serves 4

1 lb (450 g) fennel bulbs (2 large
   or 4 small)
3 tablespoons pitted Castelvetrano
   olives, torn by hand or coarsely
   chopped
2 tablespoons olive oil
½ tablespoon chardonnay vinegar
Red pepper flakes
Cracked black pepper
Zest of 1 lemon
Juice of 1–1½ lemons
Provolone cheese

Bonnie Morales ORIGIN: BELARUS

MIDWEST SALAT

My parents left the Soviet Union in 1979, as part of a wave of Russian Jews coming to America as refugees. They made their home in a tight-knit community in a suburb north of Chicago, where recent arrivals from Belarus, Ukraine, and other Soviet Republics opened their homes and hearts to each other. My mother saw this salad on a fellow immigrant's table, and it quickly made it into the regular rotation. The original incarnation featured just vegetables, mayo (the lifeblood of both Soviets and Midwesterners), and some fresh dill and scallions. I like to dress it up with toasted spices and the slight sweetness of dried fruit, creating a perfect mash-up of the traditional Midwestern mayo-based salad, and some earthy Eastern European flavors.

First, make the dressing: Pour the vegetable oil into large sauté pan and heat over high heat. When the oil is hot, but not yet smoking, add the onions. Lower the heat to medium and cook, stirring frequently, until onions are translucent, with golden and dark brown bits. Remove the onions from the pan, draining off any oil, and place them into a large mixing bowl. Once they have cooled to room temperature, add the remaining dressing ingredients to the bowl and mix well. Taste, and season with salt.

Add the broccoli, cauliflower, and Zante currants. Mix well—the dressing is intentionally very thick and will take a bit of patience to work into the florets. Taste, and season with more salt, if needed.

To serve, place the salad mixture in a shallow serving bowl (you can use a ring mold or the ring from a spring-form pan to plate your salad in a more Instagram-worthy fashion). Garnish with the spices, fried onions, and broccoli flowers (if using). If garnishing with scallions, drain them and pat dry. The ice water will have made the strips of scallion curl up like ribbons on a birthday present. Scatter them on top of your salad. This is best served the same day, but the dressing can be made up to three days in advance.

Bonnie Morales (née Frumkin) grew up in Chicago in a large Belarusian family. She trained at the Culinary Institute of America, honing her skills in Michelin-starred restaurants, including Tru, where she met her future husband and business partner, Israel Morales. In 2014, the Morales' opened Kachka, in Portland, Oregon. Kachka has received accolades from *Bon Appétit,* the *Wall Street Journal,* the *New York Times, Elle,* and *Food & Wine. Eater National* included Kachka in their "Best Restaurants in America" in 2015 and 2016. Bonnie was named one of *Tasting Table*'s "New Originals," and a "Next Generation Chef" by *Bon Appétit* in 2017. The restaurant recently launched a craft spirits line, and the Morales' first cookbook, *Kachka: A Return to Russian Cooking* (Flatiron Books), was published in November 2017.

Serves 4 to 6

2¼ cups (7 oz/200 g) broccoli florets, finely diced
2¼ cups (8 oz/225 g) cauliflower florets, finely diced
⅓ cup (1¾ oz/50 g) Zante currants

DRESSING

¼ cup (60 ml) vegetable oil
1 large onion, finely diced
2 tablespoons sesame seeds, freshly toasted
1 teaspoon poppyseeds, freshly toasted
½ teaspoon whole caraway seeds, freshly toasted
½ teaspoon whole celery seeds, freshly toasted
1 teaspoon onion powder
¼ teaspoon garlic powder
½ cup (1 oz/30 g) finely chopped dill
1 cup (240 ml) mayonnaise, preferably homemade
Kosher salt

GARNISHES

¼ teaspoon toasted sesame seeds
¼ teaspoon poppyseeds
¼ teaspoon whole caraway seeds
¼ teaspoon whole celery seeds
¼ cup (1 oz/30 g) crispy fried onions (homemade or store bought)
Handful broccoli flowers (optional)
2-3 scallions, thinly sliced lengthwise and submerged in ice water (optional)

Markus Glocker ORIGIN: AUSTRIA

ROASTED BEET LINZER

When I was growing up in Austria, Linzer Torte could be found in every *konditorei* (pastry shop). At Bâtard, we incorporate these classic flavors into our beet salad. This dish is what Bâtard and my cooking is all about—refined simplicity, complex flavors, and respect to classic techniques. While enjoying this salad, you should definitely pour yourself a glass of Grüner Veltliner to complete this journey.

Preheat oven to 375°F (200°C). Season the beets with salt and pepper, and toss with the olive oil, rosemary, thyme, and garlic. Place on a shallow baking pan. Add a few tablespoons of water, cover with aluminum foil, and roast until tender, about 45 minutes. When beets are cool, peel and set aside. Reduce the oven temperature to 350°F (180°C).

Make candied hazelnuts: Line a small baking sheet with parchment paper. In a small saucepan, combine the sugar with ¼ cup (60 ml) water. Bring to a boil, reduce the heat, and simmer until the sugar has completely dissolved. Add the hazelnuts and stir until well coated. Transfer the nuts to the baking sheet, discarding excess syrup. Roast, stirring occasionally, until golden brown, 15–20 minutes. Cool, coarsely chop, and set aside.

Season the crème fraîche with the cayenne and add salt, to taste. Mix well and set aside. Combine the dressing ingredients and set aside.

Make the linzer sable: Sift 1 cup (4½ oz/125 g) of the flour with the salt. In a separate bowl or in the bowl of a stand mixer, cream the butter with the sugar, egg, cinnamon, cloves, and citrus zests, until smooth. Add the sifted flour mixture and mix until smooth and elastic. Cover the bowl with a hot damp towel and set aside to rest for one hour.

Add the remaining 1⅓ cups (6 oz/170 g) all-purpose flour and the hazelnut flour and mix with a dough hook or your hands until smooth and elastic. Let rest again briefly.

Preheat the oven to 325°F (160°C) and line a heavy baking sheet with parchment paper. Roll the dough out until it is ⅛ inch (3 mm) thick and slice into 2 inch by ⅛ inch (5 mm by 3 mm) sticks. Place the sticks on the baking sheet and bake until golden brown, about 10 minutes.

Just before serving the salad, brush the romaine hearts lightly with olive oil and place on a hot frying pan or skillet, just until colored.

Slice the beets into wedges and toss them with the vinaigrette. Smear a little of the crème fraîche onto 4 plates. Divide the greens among the plates, and top with the beets. Garnish with the hazelnuts, currants, grilled romaine, linzer sable sticks, and freeze-dried currants, if using.

Born in Austria, **Markus Glocker** grew up working in the family hotels, where his appreciation for the culinary arts became a passion. In 2014, Markus opened Bâtard, New York, with restaurateur Drew Nieporent and managing partner John Winterman. His modern European cuisine earned three stars from *New York Magazine,* three stars from the *New York Times,* and a Michelin star, among other stellar reviews. In May 2015, Bâtard was awarded Best New Restaurant in America by the James Beard Foundation.

Serves 4

1 lb (450 g) baby beets (a mix of colors, if possible), trimmed
Salt and ground black pepper
2 tablespoons olive oil, plus more for brushing
1 rosemary sprigs
2 thyme sprigs
3 garlic cloves, peeled
¼ cup (1 oz/30 g) blanched hazelnuts
¼ cup (1¾ oz/50 g) sugar
1 cup (240 ml) crème fraîche
Pinch cayenne pepper
2 baby romaine hearts
2 cups (2½ oz/70 g) mâche salad leaves
¼ cup (1 oz/30 g) red currants
Crumbled freezed-dried currants (optional)

RASPBERRY VINAIGRETTE

½ cup (120 ml) raspberry vinegar
½ cup (120 ml) olive oil
1 cup (240 ml) canola oil

LINZER SABLE

2⅓ cups (10½ oz/300 g) all-purpose flour
1 teaspoon salt
⅔ cup (5½ oz/150 g) unsalted butter
¾ cup (5½ oz/150 g) sugar
1 large egg
½ teaspoon cinnamon
¼ teaspoon ground cloves
Zest of 1 lemon
Zest of 1 orange
1½ cups (6 oz/170 g) toasted hazelnut flour

Nick Balla ORIGIN: HUNGARY

CHEESE AND SALAMI SPOON SALAD

This salad has been a staple on our menu over the years in restaurants and at home. It has the flavors of Hungary and also reminds me of an East-Coast deli sandwich. At Duna, our San Francisco restaurant, we call it the Budapest-Brooklyn salad. My dad, Phil, made versions of this when I was growing up, and it became one of my favorite meals. No two versions were ever completely the same. He would vary the ratio of the vegetables each time he made it, for various reasons—price, quality, or seasonal availability. This approach should be the same for every batch. This recipe is a template—make it your own!

Combine all of the ingredients in a large bowl, and let stand, mixing occasionally, for 30 minutes, until the vegetables begin to give off some of their liquid. The salad should be slightly soupy. Transfer the salad to individual bowls and serve. Eat with a spoon—the juice is important!

This salad tastes best if eaten the same day it is made. Leftover salad can be stored in an airtight container in the refrigerator for up to 2 days.

Nick Balla was born in Michigan, but it was his time living in Budapest as an adolescent that left a lasting culinary mark. After graduating from the CIA Hyde Park, Nick spent extensive time in Japan, where he further learned precision and craftsmanship, before moving to San Francisco, California. In the Bay Area, he ran the kitchen at O Izakaya and Nombe, before returning to the flavors of Central Europe at Bar Tartine. There, Nick and co-chef Cortney Burns created a new type of dining in the city, one that transcended geography and celebrated the larder. Together, they published a James Beard Award–winning book, *Bar Tartine: Techniques & Recipes* (Chronicle Books, November 2014). In June 2017, Nick opened Duna, a Central European-inspired fast-casual eatery in the heart of San Francisco's Mission district.

Serves 4 to 6

12 oz (350 g) dry paprika sausage, dry chorizo, Hungarian gyulai, or pepperoni, cut into ½ inch (1 cm) cubes

8 oz (225 g) Gouda, pepper Jack, or tomme-style cheese, cut into ½ inch (1 cm) cubes

8 oz (225 g) button mushrooms, stems trimmed, quartered

8 scallions, sliced

3 yellow or green Hungarian wax peppers, stemmed, seeded, and cut into ½ inch (1 cm) cubes

1-2 green serrano or jalapeño peppers, chopped

8 oz (225 g) cherry tomatoes, halved

3 garlic cloves, minced

⅔ cup (150 ml) extra virgin olive oil

⅓ cup (75 ml) red wine vinegar

1 tablespoon chopped fresh marjoram

1 tablespoon chopped fresh dill

1 tablespoon sweet paprika

1 tablespoon hot paprika

2 teaspoons kosher salt

1 teaspoon ground black pepper

Leela Punyaratabandhu ORIGIN: THAILAND

SPICY FRUIT SALAD WITH SHRIMP

In Thailand, where I grew up, it is not uncommon to see fruit trees, such as mango, banana, papaya, or rose apple, in people's backyards. Fresh, beautiful, and delicious tropical fruits are available all year round. The variety is immense! Living in the United States means that I don't have access to most of those tropical fruits in their fresh state, but it also means I can enjoy so many great non-tropical fruits that I didn't grow up eating. With the bounty of this great land and some creativity, recreating the flavors of Thailand in my Chicago kitchen is easy and fun.

This is a spicy, semi-savory fruit salad inspired by a fruit salad that I often make and eat in Thailand. It carries the Thai flavors of fresh lime, fish sauce, and chilies that I love and crave. Instead of tropical fruits, however, it is made with fruits that you can find anywhere in the US. I often bring this salad to summer and early-fall picnics and it is always a hit among my friends.

Serves 6

1 lb (450 g) large shrimp, peeled
   and deveined
1 teaspoon salt
1 Granny Smith apple
1 sweet red apple, such as Washington,
   Fuji, or Gala
1 cup (6 oz/170 g) cubed fresh
   pineapple (do not use canned)
2 tablespoons fresh lime juice,
   plus more to taste
1 medium cucumber
8 oz (225 g) strawberries, hulled and
   halved (or quartered if large)
1½ cups (8 oz/225 g) grapes
1 teaspoon Thai fish sauce or salt,
   plus more to taste
Grated Thai palm sugar or light
   brown sugar
Cayenne pepper or red pepper flakes
¾ cup (3½ oz/100 g) roasted
   unsalted cashews

Fill a medium saucepan halfway with water and bring to a boil over high heat. Meanwhile, slice the shrimp crosswise into ½ inch (1 cm) pieces. When the water boils, stir in the salt and lower the heat so that the water is no longer bubbling, but only steaming. Stir in the shrimp and poach gently until they are firm and pink. Drain well and set aside to cool.

Meanwhile, quarter each apple lengthwise and halve each quarter lengthwise. Cut each slice crosswise into ½ inch (1 cm) pieces and place in a large mixing bowl. Add the pineapple cubes to the bowl, along with the lime juice. Mix very well to ensure that every apple piece is coated with juice; the acid keeps them from turning brown. Cover.

Working quickly, quarter the cucumber lengthwise and slice off the seeds. Cut the spears crosswise into ½ inch (1 cm) slices and add them to the mixing bowl. Add the cooked shrimp, strawberries, and grapes.

Season with a little bit of the fish sauce, starting with 1 teaspoon, and adding more according to taste. Add lime juice and palm sugar to taste, until you get a flavor that is equally salty, sour, and sweet. (If the fruits are in season and very sweet, you may need more lime juice, and no palm sugar at all. When dealing with fruits, you will have to play it by ear.) When the salad is seasoned to your liking, sprinkle with the cayenne or red pepper flakes, and toss well. Top with the cashews and serve immediately.

Born and raised in Bangkok, Thailand, **Leela Punyaratabandhu** came to the United States for school. She writes about Thai food on her award-winning website, *She Simmers*, and has authored two books: *Bangkok: Recipes and Stories from the Heart of Thailand* and *Simple Thai Food: Classic Recipes from the Thai Home Kitchen*. Leela has been named one of the 100 Greatest Home Cooks of All Time by *Epicurious*. She splits her time between Chicago and Bangkok.

Barbara Abdeni Massaad ORIGIN: LEBANON

LEBANESE PEASANT SALAD
Fattoush

I make this salad with whatever seasonal produce I find. That's the beauty of it! I can buy wholesome local produce and improvise. Stale bread that has been lying around a bit too long is perfect for frying or baking, and is an essential ingredient in this recipe (throwing away bread is *haram*—a sacrilege in our culture). The vegetables can be roughly chopped without too much fuss, peasant-style. Look for fresh sumac made from 100% ground sumac berries. Store sumac in your pantry for one year only (not a day more; please label all your spices). *Fattoush* will burst with flavors with a sprinkle of fresh ground sumac. Make friends with your Middle Eastern grocer; he'll give you the best of the batch.

Put the lettuce in a large salad bowl (the prettiest and largest bowl you have). Add the rest of the salad ingredients (or experiment with what you have available!). This is where your senses will start to tingle.

Bake, grill, or deep-fry the pieces of bread. Deep-frying is traditional—you can't beat that taste! Set aside.

The dressing is simple: Crush the garlic with a pinch of salt using a mortar and a pestle. Mash it hard! Add the lemon juice, pomegranate molasses or balsamic vinegar, and finally, the purest extra virgin olive oil. Taste and add more salt, if needed. Pour the dressing onto the salad.

Sprinkle with sumac, and toss. Add the bread and toss again. Serve immediately or the bread will get soggy.

Barbara Abdeni Massaad is a food writer, TV host, and cookbook author. Born in Beirut, Lebanon, she moved to Florida at a young age, gaining her first culinary experience helping her father in their family-owned Lebanese restaurant, Kebabs and Things. She went on to train with renowned chefs at Lebanese, Italian, and French restaurants. Her first cookbook, *Man'oushé: Inside the Lebanese Street-Corner Bakery*, won The Lebanese Academy of Gastronomy Award in 2009. Her book *Soup for Syria: Recipes to Celebrate Our Shared Humanity* gathered recipes from prominent chefs to help raise funds for food and medical relief efforts for Syrian refugees. Her latest book, *Mouneh: Preserving Foods for the Lebanese Pantry* (Interlink, 2017) continues her quest to discover and preserve Lebanese culinary heritage. She is a founding member of Slow Food Beirut and a member of Les Ambassadeurs du Pain.

Serves 4 to 6

1 head romaine lettuce, cut into strips
1 bunch flat-leaf parsley, coarsely chopped
½ bunch mint, leaves stripped
4–5 Lebanese or Persian cucumbers, sliced
3–4 medium tomatoes, cut into wedges
5–6 radishes, sliced
1 medium green bell pepper, coarsely chopped
1 medium red bell pepper, coarsely chopped
1–2 bunches purslane, leaves stripped, or use mâche or watercress
3–4 cups (4 oz/115 g) arugula
1 medium onion, sliced
2–3 scallions, finely chopped (optional)

GARNISH
1–2 loaves Arabic bread or pita, cut into squares
Oil, for frying (optional)
1–2 tablespoons good-quality sumac

DRESSING
1–2 garlic cloves, crushed
Fine sea salt
Juice of ½ lemon
¼ cup (60 ml) pomegranate molasses or balsamic vinegar
½ cup (120 ml) extra virgin olive oil

SOUPS

José Andrés ORIGIN: SPAIN

TICHI'S GAZPACHO

I am originally from the north of Spain, while my wife Patricia ("Tichi") is from Andalucía, in the south. The south is known for gazpacho, a refreshing chilled tomato soup, and Tichi's recipe is one of the best in the world! In the summer we always have a pitcher of it chilling in the fridge for our family, friends, and last-minute guests. I once found a recipe for gazpacho in an early-American cookbook, *The Virginia Housewife* by Mary Randolph, first published in 1824. This was such an amazing discovery to me, as it exemplified a long history of Spanish influence on American cuisine. So now every time I have gazpacho, I think, of course, of Tichi's childhood and upbringing, but also of the legacy of immigrants on American culinary traditions.

In a blender or food processor, combine the cucumbers, pepper, tomatoes, garlic, vinegar, sherry, olive oil, and salt (you may need to work in batches). Purée until everything is well blended into a thick orange liquid. If necessary, add ½ to 1 cup (120 to 240 ml) water to adjust to your preferred consistency, and pulse to combine.

Pour the gazpacho through a medium strainer into a pitcher and refrigerate for at least 30 minutes.

Prepare the garnish: Preheat the oven to 400°F (200°C). Cut the bread into 1 inch (2 cm) cubes and toss in a mixing bowl with 2 tablespoons of the olive oil. Spread the bread on a baking sheet and bake on the middle rack until golden brown, about 7 minutes. Set the croutons aside to cool.

When you are ready to serve, remove the gazpacho from the refrigerator and give it a stir. Put a few croutons, cherry tomato halves, and diced cucumbers in each bowl and pour the gazpacho over them. Drizzle each bowl with the remaining olive oil and sprinkle with sea salt.

Serves 6 to 8

1 cucumber, peeled, seeded, and chopped
1 green bell pepper, seeded and diced
3 lb (1.4 kg) ripe plum tomatoes
2 garlic cloves, peeled
¼ cup (60 ml) sherry vinegar
½ cup (120 ml) Oloroso sherry
¾ cup (175 ml) Spanish extra virgin olive oil
2 teaspoons sea salt, plus more to taste

GARNISHES

2 slices rustic bread, each 1 inch (2 cm) thick
¼ cup (60 ml) Spanish extra virgin olive oil
12 cherry tomatoes, halved
½ cucumber, diced

José Andrés, named one of *Time*'s "100 Most Influential People" and Outstanding Chef by the James Beard Foundation, is an internationally recognized culinary innovator, author, educator, television personality, humanitarian, and chef/owner of ThinkFoodGroup. A pioneer of Spanish tapas in the United States, he is known for his avant-garde cuisine and his award-winning group of 27 restaurants throughout the country and beyond. His innovative minibar by José Andrés earned two Michelin stars in 2016 and with that, José is the only chef globally that has both a Michelin two-star restaurant and four Bib Gourmands. José's work has earned numerous awards, including the 2015 National Humanities Medal, and he is one of the 12 distinguished recipients of the award from the National Endowment for the Humanities.

Ryan Lachaine ORIGIN: CANADA, UKRAINE

BORSCHT

Making borscht is one of my earliest childhood memories of being in the kitchen. My Ukrainian grandmother and mother would make it, and I can remember my grandfather and my dad being really excited about it. Now when I go to Winnipeg, I want it all the time. If my mom doesn't have it, I go a restaurant called Ludas in the North End. It's amazing.

Preheat oven to 400°F (200°C). Place the beets on a baking sheet and roast until tender, 60 to 80 minutes. Once cooled, remove the skin, chop the flesh, and set aside.

Place the oil in a large deep sauté pan or pot over medium heat. Add the onion and garlic and sauté until translucent but not browned, 3 to 5 minutes. Add the beets, dill, and tomatoes. Increase heat to medium-high and sauté until the dill wilts and the beets turn the onions purple, about 3 minutes. Add the beef stock, maple syrup, vinegar, and bay leaf. Adjust the heat to bring the mixture to a simmer. Cover and cook until all the vegetables are tender, 10 to 15 minutes. Taste and add salt to your liking.

Remove from heat and let cool. Discard the bay leaf and dill. Once cooled, transfer the mixture to a blender or food processor and blend until smooth. Strain through a chinois or sieve, and season with salt, if needed. Garnish with shaved horseradish, a dollop of crème fraîche, and a sprig of dill.

Serves 4

2 lb (1 kg) beets, washed and scrubbed
1 tablespoon canola oil
1 medium onion, diced
4 garlic cloves, thinly sliced
1 bunch dill, tied with twine, plus a few springs to garnish
¾ cup (6 oz/170 g) canned chopped tomatoes
3 cups (700 ml) beef stock
2 tablespoons maple syrup
2-3 tablespoons red wine vinegar
1 bay leaf
Salt
Shaved horseradish, to serve (optional)
Crème fraîche, to serve

Ryan Lachaine is executive chef and co-owner of Riel, in Houston, Texas. His first culinary education began at the apron strings of his Ukrainian mother and grandmother in his family home in Manitoba, Canada. He trained under Chef Bryan Caswell at Stella Sola, before staging at some of the country's top restaurants, earning him an induction into *Eater*'s 2013 Class of Young Guns. He named Riel after Louis Riel, the founder of Manitoba and leader of the Métis community and the movement to preserve the group's native lands, culture, and languages. Ryan chose Riel to represent his own Canadian heritage and the many cultures that Riel sought to bring together, something Ryan does on the plates of his restaurant.

Serge Madikians ORIGIN: ARMENIA, IRAN

ARMENIAN-STYLE CHILLED YOGURT SOUP
Ja'jick

I grew up eating this soup. Whenever I visit family or friends, especially in the hot summer months, one version or another of this soup is served. I've changed and perfected the technique a bit and I've now been serving this soup at my restaurant, Serevan, for years. I prefer to make the soup with small Persian cucumbers, which I grow in my garden; in my opinion, they work best, but in case they are not available in your local food store, you can use English cucumbers.

Peel one-third of the cucumbers, remove the seeds, and finely dice; then set them aside in the refrigerator.

Peel and coarsely chop the remaining cucumbers. Place half of these in a blender with the water and 1 tablespoon of the salt, and blend until puréed. With the blender running, add the remaining coarsely chopped cucumbers, and the shallots and garlic, and continue to blend for at least 1 minute.

Place the yogurt in a bowl large enough to comfortably hold double its size. Add the blended cucumber mixture and mix well, using a whisk. Add the remaining 1 tablespoon salt, and, whisking continuously, slowly drizzle in the olive oil and the lemon juice. Taste and adjust the seasoning to your liking, and add the cayenne, if desired.

Add the diced cucumbers and the herbs and mix well. Ladle into chilled soup bowls and garnish with a drizzle of olive oil, if desired.

Serves 6 to 8

2 lb (1 kg) cucumbers (3 English
    or 15 Persian), peeled
¼ cup (60 ml) water
2 tablespoons kosher salt, or to taste
2 shallots, peeled and quartered
2 garlic cloves
4 cups (2 lb/1 kg) plain whole milk
    yogurt
½ cup (120 ml) extra virgin olive oil,
    plus extra to garnish
Juice of 1 lemon
Pinch cayenne pepper (optional)
10 dill sprigs, stems removed,
    finely chopped
10 mint sprigs, stems removed,
    finely chopped
10 cilantro sprigs, stems removed,
    finely chopped

Serge Madikians is chef/owner of Serevan in the Hudson Valley, New York. After a childhood in pre-revolutionary Tehran, he came to the US for his undergraduate studies in California and graduate school at the New School in New York, where he studied public policy and economics. While working for the City of New York, he took night classes at the International Culinary Center, going on to work with renowned chefs Jean-George Vongerichten and David Bouley. After opening his own restaurant in 2005, he was named Best Chef in the Hudson Valley by *Hudson Valley Magazine* and was a semifinalist for the James Beard Awards' Best Chef in the Northeast, both for two years running. The cuisine at Serevan celebrates the abundance of the Hudson Valley and Serevan's own gardens, through the prism of Iranian and Iranian-Armenian flavor spectrums and cultural heritage.

Marco Canora ORIGIN: ITALY

CRANBERRY BEAN SOUP WITH FARRO

My mom was born and raised in Lucca in Tuscany, a region famous for farro and soups. I'm sharing a recipe for a super-traditional Tuscan soup. To be honest, I'm not that interested in innovation; there are things that have stood the test of the time for a reason. As a chef, I like to focus on quality and execution, respecting traditions and keeping that lineage alive. I feel that more respect and attention must be given to timeless classics. You will need to soak the beans overnight.

In a large soup pot, heat the olive oil over high heat. When the oil is hot and slides easily across the pan, add the onions, carrots, celery, garlic, and anchovies, and a couple of pinches of salt. Cook, stirring occasionally, until the vegetables are soft and lightly browned, about 10 minutes.

Add the tomato paste, stirring well to coat the vegetables. Reduce the heat to medium-low and cook, stirring occasionally, until the mixture has thickened and darkened, about 10 minutes.

Stir in the beans, measured water, bouquet garni, and a couple of pinches of salt. Bring to a boil over high heat, then reduce to a gentle simmer (there should only be a little movement in the liquid). Cook, stirring occasionally, until the beans are soft and creamy, 1 to 2 hours. (This is a forgiving soup, so don't worry about overcooking it.)

In a small pot, cook the farro according to the package instructions, until it is just cooked.

When the beans are cooked, remove the bouquet garni. Working in batches, purée the soup in a blender and add to a clean pot over medium heat. Add salt and pepper to taste and adjust the consistency with more water or broth, if needed.

To serve, place 3 tablespoons of farro in each serving bowl. Ladle the soup over it, and garnish with fresh thyme, Parmesan, and a few dots of olive oil.

Marco Canora is an Italian-American chef, restaurateur, and author of three cookbooks. His restaurant, Hearth, in New York's East Village, quickly became a culinary destination, even before its reinvention in 2016. Brodo kicked off America's bone broth craze and continues to be an industry leader. His recent venture, Zadie's Oyster Room, opened in 2016, is an ode to turn-of-the-century oyster houses. In 2017, Marco won the James Beard Award for Best Chef, New York. His appreciation for delicious food has been a part of him since his childhood in upstate New York, where he enjoyed the freshest herbs and vegetables from the garden and cooked with his mother for hours on end. When he's not in the kitchen, Marco enjoys time with his family in Martha's Vineyard.

Serves 8

3 tablespoons extra virgin olive oil, plus more to serve
2 medium onions, chopped
3 small carrots, peeled and chopped
3 celery stalks, chopped
8 garlic cloves, peeled and smashed
3 olive oil-packed anchovy fillets
Sea salt
1 tablespoon tomato paste
2¼ cups (1 lb/450 g) dried cranberry beans, soaked overnight, drained
10 cups (2.5 liters) broth or water
Bouquet garni (a few sprigs each of thyme, rosemary, and sage, tied with a string), plus extra thyme to garnish
¾ cup (5 oz/140 g) farro
Ground black pepper
Freshly grated Parmigiano Reggiano, to serve

Hari Nayak ORIGIN: INDIA
LENTIL AND SPINACH SOUP
Dal Palak

This recipe is inspired by the Indian comfort food *dal palak*, which means lentils with spinach, though you can use chard or kale as alternative options. I often make lentil soups, called *dal* in India, using whatever vegetables or greens are available in my refrigerator. The lentils act as a natural thickening agent, creating a nourishing, flavorful, healthy one-bowl meal to savor. This soup is best served over a bowl of warm rice or with naan bread. Its beauty is in its rustic simplicity.

Heat the oil in a large saucepan over medium heat. Add the cumin seeds—they should sizzle upon contact. Add the onion, garlic, ginger, garam masala, and turmeric, and cook, stirring constantly, until the spices are fragrant, about 1 minute. Add the tomato and cook for another 30 seconds.

Add the lentils and 2 cups (480 ml) water, and bring to a boil over medium-high heat. Reduce the heat to low, cover, and simmer gently until the lentils are tender, about 15 to 20 minutes. Check after 10 to 15 minutes and add up to 1 cup (240 ml) more water if you want the soup to be thinner. If you prefer a smooth soup, purée the mixture using a hand blender.

Stir in the spinach, coconut milk, and salt, to taste. Cover, and simmer until the spinach is cooked, about 3 minutes more. Serve hot, garnished with the cilantro, if desired.

Hari Nayak is a chef, cookbook author, restaurateur, and consultant born in Udupi, a small town in South India famous for vegetarian cooking. He has authored six cookbooks and is recognized as a pioneer of modern Indian cuisine and for his vision is to bring Indian culture and cuisine to the forefront of the global culinary map. He lives in New Jersey.

Serves 4

1 tablespoon vegetable oil
1 teaspoon cumin seeds
1 medium red onion, chopped
2 large garlic cloves, crushed
1 teaspoon ground ginger
½ teaspoon garam masala
¼ teaspoon turmeric
1 small tomato, chopped
1 cup (7 oz/200 g) yellow or red lentils, rinsed and drained
3 cups (3½ oz/100 g) fresh spinach leaves, washed and chopped, or 1 cup (5½ oz/150 g) frozen chopped spinach, thawed
½ cup (120 ml) coconut milk
Salt
2 tablespoons chopped fresh cilantro (optional)

Ivan Garcia ORIGIN: MEXICO

GARIBALDI-STYLE POZOLE ROJO

Pozole Rojo Estilo Garibaldi

This is one of the most traditional and representative dishes of my country. Mexican families usually prepare this dish to celebrate important dates or events, like our Independence Day, Mother's Day, a loved one's birthday, sometimes a divorce! It features two ingredients that are key in the Mexican gastronomy: corn and hot chili peppers. This recipe is easily doubled if you're feeding a crowd.

In a large stockpot, bring 10 cups (2.5 liters) water to a boil. Add the meat, onion, garlic, cloves, peppercorns, bay leaves, and salt. Reduce the heat and simmer, covered, until the pork is very tender, 50 minutes. Strain the stock, reserving the meat and discarding the aromatics.

In a large saucepan, bring 4 cups (1 liter) water to a boil over high heat. Add the chilies and boil, uncovered, for 8 minutes, until tender. In a blender, purée the chilies and liquid until no pieces are visible (you may need to do this in batches).

In a large pot, combine the reserved stock with the chili salsa and bring to a boil over medium heat. Reduce the heat to low, add the reserved meat and the hominy, and simmer for 20 minutes.

Serve with the lettuce, radish, avocado, and lime wedges on the side, so that each person can garnish as they like.

Ivan Garcia is chef and owner of Mesa Coyoacan, Zona Rosa, and Guadalupe Inn in Brooklyn. He was born and raised in the Coyoacan neighborhood of Mexico City and moved to New York in 2000, honing his personal style in some of the city's top restaurants. Ivan holds great reverence for authentic Mexican dishes. His style celebrates his heritage and highlights the diverse flavors and ingredients ubiquitous in Mexican cuisine.

Serves 6 to 8

2 lb (1 kg) boneless pork shoulder, cut into 2 inch (5 cm) pieces (add a bone to flavor the stock, if desired)
1 white onion, coarsely chopped
3 small garlic cloves
3 whole cloves
3 whole black peppercorns
3 bay leaves
1 tablespoon salt
2 dried guajillo chilies, stemmed, seeds shaken out
2 dried ancho chilies, stemmed, seeds shaken out
2 dried chile de árbol peppers, stemmed, seeds shaken out
One to two 29 oz (825 g) cans white hominy corn, rinsed and drained

TO SERVE
Shredded romaine lettuce
Radish slices
Avocado slices
Lime wedges

Alicia Maher ORIGIN: EL SALVADOR

SALVADORAN SHRIMP SOUP
Sopa de Camarones

This traditional Salvadoran soup graces the cover of my cookbook, *Delicious El Salvador*. I chose this dish because is one of the most popular soups in El Salvador, and it reminds me of my *abuela*. There are different versions of this recipe—one with cream, added just before serving, and one with beaten eggs cooked into the soup. This soup reflects the fusion of Spanish ingredients like onions, carrots, garlic, and cilantro, with local ingredients like seafood, tomatoes, green pepper, and potatoes. That is the special aspect of immigration—it brings the world together.

My grandmother was from the town of Ahuachapan. I lived with her for about two years, and she took me shopping almost every day in the local *mercado*. With the closest beach only nineteen miles away, we enjoyed an abundance of fresh and inexpensive seafood. I would watch her face turn serious when choosing the right shrimp for the soup. She was good at haggling too; no one could say no to that beautiful smile!

In a large pot over high heat, heat the butter or oil until very hot. Sauté the shrimp until just pink, 1 to 2 minutes, and transfer to a plate, leaving the oil in the pot. Add the onions, garlic, cilantro, tomato, and green pepper to the pot, and sauté for about 1 minute, stirring.

Add the water or stock, bouillon powder (if using), and salt, and bring to a boil. Stir in the potato cubes and carrot slices, cover, reduce the heat to medium, and cook for 10 minutes.

Return the shrimp to the pot and simmer until they are cooked through and the vegetables are tender, about 5 minutes.

Add the cream, if using, stir, and remove from the heat. Taste and add salt, if needed. Serve hot, with a squeeze of lemon juice.

Serves 4 to 6

¼ cup (2 oz/60 g) butter or vegetable oil
1 lb (450 g) medium shrimp (about 30), peeled, deveined, tails left intact
1 large onion, finely chopped
2 large garlic cloves, minced
½ cup (¾ oz/20g) chopped cilantro
1 large tomato, chopped
1 small green bell pepper, chopped
8 cups (2 liters) fish or vegetable stock, or water
1 tablespoon low-sodium shrimp or chicken bouillon powder (optional)
1 teaspoon salt, or to taste
1 small potato, peeled and cubed
2 medium carrots, peeled and sliced
½ cup (120 ml) heavy cream (optional)
Lemon wedges, to serve

Alicia Maher is the author of *Delicious El Salvador*, which won Gourmand's Best First Cookbook award in 2014. She was born and raised in El Salvador and has made California her home since 1986. She teaches cooking classes privately, and at Whole Foods Markets in Los Angeles. Known as "El Salvador's Culinary Ambassador," she will soon launch the Spanish edition of *Delicious El Salvador*, and is working on her second Salvadoran cookbook. She lives in California with her husband, Joseph Maher, and their three sons.

Ana Patuleia Ortins ORIGIN: PORTUGAL

PORTUGUESE BEAN SOUP
Sopa de Feijão

As a young girl, I learned to cook the traditional fare of my cultural heritage by my father's side. I learned to appreciate the value of using the freshest ingredients I could lay my hands on, and to improvise with what I had on hand. I learned food was not to be wasted. These are lessons that have influenced my cooking to this day, and which I have passed to my own children.

The simple and traditional *sopa de feijão*, in the style of my father's hometown of Galveias, is one of the first soups my father taught me to make. He would set a colander over the soup pot and let me force the beans through the holes, using just a fork and some water. The lighter bean broth and the additional flavor of cilantro sets this version apart from other recipes. As a variation, you can use white kidney beans (my grandfather's favorite), in place of the red beans. And flouting tradition, my father often added a small chunk of dry-cured sausage to the pot. You will need to soak the beans overnight.

Serves 6

1¼ cups (8 oz/225 g) dried red kidney or roman beans, soaked overnight in water to cover by 2 inches (5 cm)

8 cups (2 liters) water or vegetable stock, plus more if needed

¼ cup (60 ml) extra virgin olive oil

3 garlic cloves, finely chopped

1 bay leaf

14 oz (400 g) kale or collard leaves, trimmed of the thick center stems, coarsely chopped

4 oz (115 g) Portuguese chouriço or Spanish chorizo, thinly sliced (optional)

1 tablespoon finely chopped cilantro, or to taste

1 tablespoon coarse salt, or to taste

½ teaspoon ground black pepper, or to taste

Drain and rinse the beans. Place the beans in a large stockpot with 8 cups (2 liters) water or vegetable stock. Cover and bring to a boil. Reduce the heat to medium-low and simmer for 1 hour or until the beans are very tender, and can be easily mashed with a fork.

Using a wooden spoon, press about half of the beans against the side of the pot to thicken the broth, leaving some beans whole. Alternatively, push half of the beans through a food mill, colander, or sieve set over a bowl, discarding the skins, then return the bean purée to the pot.

Add the olive oil, garlic, and bay leaf, and return the soup to a boil. Add the kale, sausage (if using), cilantro, salt, and pepper. Re-cover the pot, reduce the heat, and simmer for about 10 to 15 minutes, until the kale is tender, but not mushy. If the soup is too thick at this point, add water or stock to thin it to your liking. This soup can be served simply with crusty country bread and olives.

Ana Patuleia Ortins is a culinary instructor and chef, and author of two cookbooks, *Portuguese Homestyle Cooking* and *Authentic Portuguese Cooking*. She is a first-generation descendant of Portuguese immigrants from the small town of Galveias in the Alto Alentejo province of Portugal. She lives in Massachusetts.

Joanne Chang ORIGIN: TAIWAN

MAMA CHANG'S HOT AND SOUR SOUP

All of the bright and peppery flavors of the hot and sour soup you get at a restaurant, with none of the gloop! Ground pork is a bit untraditional for this soup, but it makes the preparation ultra quick. Wood ear mushrooms, sometimes labeled tree fungus (now there's an appetizing name), are a standard addition, but they can be hard to find unless you live near an Asian grocery store. I substitute easy-to-find button mushrooms, which don't have the same crunch and add a nice earthy flavor. Egg, not flavorless cornstarch, acts as the thickener, allowing the flavors of pork, sesame, vinegar, and pepper to come shining through. My mom used to whip this up as a quick lunch for my brother and me, and I have taught it to the chefs at Flour so that they can offer it as a daily soup special. It always sells out and Mom is thrilled to be part of the Flour menu.

In a large saucepan, heat the oil over medium-high heat. Add the garlic, ginger, scallions, and pork and cook for about a minute, stirring occasionally. Break up the pork into smaller pieces but don't worry about completely breaking it down. Add chicken stock and bring to a simmer.

Cut the tofu into ½ in (1 cm) cubes and add it to broth. Add the mushrooms, sugar, rice wine vinegar, soy sauce, black pepper, sesame oil, and sriracha, and bring back to a simmer over medium-high heat. Adjust the seasoning with more sriracha or vinegar if you want it hotter or sourer.

Whisk the eggs together in a small bowl and, with the soup at a steady simmer, whisk them slowly into the broth.

Bring the broth back to a simmer. Divide it among four serving bowls and garnish each with a little of the sesame oil, chopped scallions, and white pepper. Serve immediately.

Joanne Chang was an honors graduate of Harvard College with a degree in Applied Mathematics and Economics, when she left a career as a management consultant to enter the world of professional cooking. She is the chef and co-owner of Flour Bakery + Café, with seven locations in the Boston area, and Myers + Chang. She is the winner of the James Beard Award for Outstanding Baker, as well as the author of *Flour: Spectacular Recipes from Boston's Flour Bakery + Cafe*; *Flour, too: Indispensable Recipes for the Café's Most Loved Sweets & Savories*; *Baking with Less Sugar*; and *Myers + Chang at Home: Recipes from the Beloved Boston Eatery*. She is currently working on her fifth book, *Pastry Love*.

Serves 4

2 tablespoons vegetable or canola oil
1 garlic clove, minced
1 tablespoon finely chopped
    fresh ginger
4 scallions, finely chopped, plus
    more to garnish
8 oz (225 g) ground pork
4 cups (1 liter) chicken stock
1 lb (450 g) block soft or firm tofu
    (not silken and not extra firm)
4–5 medium button mushrooms,
    thinly sliced
2 teaspoons sugar
½ cup (120 ml) rice wine vinegar,
    plus more to taste
3 tablespoons soy sauce
1 teaspoon ground black pepper
1 tablespoon sesame oil, plus
    more to garnish
2 teaspoons sriracha, plus more to taste
2 eggs
White pepper, to garnish

BEEF NOODLE SOUP
Pho Bo

When you eat a bowl of soup in Vietnam, you experience almost everything, culinarily speaking, that the Vietnamese value. The stock is flavorful and light. Every bowl includes a texturally interesting mix of soft ingredients, crunchy elements, and chewy bits, flavored with aromatics. I have included my beef stock recipe, but you can use any good-quality beef stock, if preferred.

Place the brisket in a large pot and add the stock. Bring to a boil over high heat, then lower the heat until the liquid is at a vigorous simmer. Cook the brisket for 30 to 45 minutes, or until cooked through. (To check, transfer the brisket to a plate and poke with the tip of a chopstick; the juices should run clear.)

Half-fill a large bowl or pot with ice water. Transfer the cooked brisket to the ice water, reserving the cooking liquid. This will stop the cooking, and give the meat a firmer texture. When the brisket is completely cool, remove from the water, pat dry, and thinly slice against the grain. Set aside.

Return the stock to a boil over high heat. Taste for seasoning and add fish sauce, if needed.

To ready the garnishes, arrange the basil, bean sprouts, lime wedges, and peppers on a platter. Divide the cooked rice noodles evenly between warmed soup bowls. Top with the brisket slices and then with the raw beef slices, dividing them evenly. Ladle the hot stock over the top, and top with the scallions. Serve immediately, accompanied with the platter of garnishes and the sriracha and hoisin sauces alongside.

Serves 6

1 lb (450 g) beef brisket
12 cups (2.8 liters) beef stock
  (recipe right)
Fish sauce (optional)
1 lb (450 g) package dried wide rice
  noodles, cooked according to the
  package directions
12 oz (350 g) beef top round,
  thinly sliced (optional)
1 bunch scallions, trimmed and
  thinly sliced

GARNISHES
Thai basil sprigs
Mung bean sprouts
Lime wedges
Jalapeño peppers, stemmed
  and thinly sliced
Sriracha
Hoisin sauce

BEEF STOCK

Preheat the oven to 350°F (180°C). Place the onion and ginger on a rimmed baking sheet and roast until the onion is soft and beginning to ooze, about 1 hour. Remove from the oven and let the onion and ginger cool until they can be handled. Peel the onion and cut it in half. Slice the unpeeled ginger into ¼ inch (6 mm) thick coins.

While the onion and ginger are roasting, blanch the oxtails, neck bones, and shanks in your largest stockpot: To ensure the pot is large enough to blanch the bones without boiling over, put them in the pot and add water to cover by 1 inch (2 cm). Then remove the bones and bring the water to a boil over high heat. When it is at a rolling boil, add the bones, return the water to a boil, and boil for 3 minutes. Drain the contents of the pot through a colander and rinse the bones under cold running water. Rinse the pot and return the blanched oxtails, neck bones, and shanks to the pot. Add the marrowbones.

Add the onion halves, ginger slices, salt, sugar, and 8 quarts (7.5 liters) fresh water to the pot and bring to a boil over high heat, skimming off any scum that forms on the surface. Lower the heat to a gentle simmer, and cook for 4 hours, skimming as needed. Add the pepper, cinnamon, star anise, clove, and cardamom, and continue cooking, skimming occasionally, for 1 hour more.

Remove from the heat and, using a slotted spoon, discard the large solids. Strain the stock through a fine-mesh sieve into a large container, let sit for a few minutes (or refrigerate overnight), then skim most of the fat from the surface (leave some, as it gives the stock a better flavor and mouth feel). Use immediately, or let cool completely, then transfer to practical-size airtight containers and refrigerate for up to 3 days or freeze for up to 3 months.

(Pictured on page 67)

Makes about 6 quarts/5.6 liters

1 large yellow onion, unpeeled
3 inch (8 cm) piece fresh ginger
2 lb (1 kg) oxtails, cut in 2 to 3 inch (5 to 8 cm) pieces
2 lb (1 kg) beef neck bones
2 lb (1 kg) beef shank bones
2 lb (1 kg) beef marrowbones
1 tablespoon kosher salt
1 oz (30 g) light brown palm sugar or 2 tablespoons light brown sugar
1 teaspoon ground white pepper
3 inch (8 cm) piece Chinese cinnamon
1 whole star anise
1 whole clove
1 black cardamom pod (optional)

Charles Phan is the inventor of modern Vietnamese cuisine in America and executive chef and owner of the Slanted Door family of restaurants. Born in Da Lat, Vietnam, the Phan family relocated just before the fall of Saigon in 1975, spending two years in Guam before settling in San Francisco. Charles opened his first restaurant, The Slanted Door, in 1995. In 2014, the restaurant was named Outstanding Restaurant by the James Beard Foundation. His current restaurants in San Francisco are Out the Door, OTD, and Hard Water. Upcoming projects are Rice and Bones at Wurster Hall UC Berkeley, and The Slanted Door in other urban areas. Charles has been featured on Food Network's *Iron Chef America* and Mark Bittman's *How to Cook Everything*. In 2004, he won the James Beard Foundation's Best Chef, California. He is author of two cookbooks, *Vietnamese Home Cooking*, and *The Slanted Door*, both winning IACP cookbook awards. He is a leader in the San Francisco food community and has participated in countless charitable events.

VEGETABLES

Claus Meyer ORIGIN: DENMARK

GREEN POTATO SMØRREBRØD

If I only had one hour left to live, a potato with mayonnaise would be one of my last bites. This open-face rye sandwich is my ode to potato salad. In my native Denmark, *smørrebrød* became the default option for an inexpensive, satisfying lunch in the late 19th century, when factory workers began eating their midday meal away from home. Workers piled the few leftovers they had onto cheap, filling *rugbrød* (Danish rye bread), and hoped munching on a few open-faced sandwiches would satisfy them until dinner. From this, a gastronomic tradition was born. I add fresh dill, pickled pearl onions, and potato chips to my version for crunch and dimension.

In a medium saucepan, combine the apple cider vinegar with the sugar and 1 cup (240 ml) water, and bring to a boil. Add the pearl onions and a pinch of salt. Transfer to a large heatproof jar or tub and let cool completely. Refrigerate overnight (or for up to 5 days).

In a medium saucepan, cover the potatoes, lemon zest, dill sprigs, and peppercorns with water and bring to a boil. Add a generous pinch of salt, and simmer until just tender, about 20 minutes. Remove from the heat and let the potatoes cool in the cooking liquid, about 30 minutes. Drain well and discard the aromatics. Cut the potatoes into ¼ inch (6 mm) thick slices.

In a small bowl or food processor, whisk or pulse the mayonnaise with the chopped dill, mustard, and white wine vinegar. Season with salt.

Cut 4 of the pickled pearl onions in half and separate the layers. Reserve the remaining onions for another use.

Spread the rye bread with butter and arrange the potato slices on top. Dollop the dill mayonnaise on the potatoes, and season with salt and pepper. Garnish with the pickled onion petals, shallot or onion slices, dill sprigs, and potato chips; serve immediately.

Claus Meyer is the initiator of the New Nordic Cuisine movement, co-founder of the Nordic Food Lab, and the now legendary Noma. Claus has hosted several Danish and international cooking shows and written numerous cookbooks. Believing in food as a driver for social change, he established the Melting Pot Foundation in 2010, which initiated a cooking school project in Danish state prisons; and a cooking school in La Paz, Bolivia, which provides culinary education to impoverished Bolivians and serves as a fine-dining restaurant, GUSTU. This summer, Claus's newest social project is the Brownsville Community Culinary Center, a culinary school, cafeteria, bakery, and community center. In 2016 he opened Agern and the Great Northern Food Hall in Grand Central Terminal, bringing the culinary concepts, flavors, and ideas rooted in the history and landscapes of Nordic countries to New York City.

Serves 4

1 cup (240 ml) apple cider vinegar
¾ cup (5½ oz/150 g) sugar
8 oz (225 g) pearl onions, peeled, or
    frozen pearl onions, thawed
Kosher salt and ground black pepper
6 oz (170 g) fingerling potatoes
Five 3 inch (8 cm) strips of lemon zest
3 dill sprigs, plus more to garnish
¼ teaspoon whole black peppercorns
½ cup (120 ml) mayonnaise
2 tablespoons finely chopped dill
1 teaspoon Dijon mustard
1 teaspoon white wine vinegar
4 slices of dense rye bread
Unsalted European-style butter,
    softened, for spreading
1 shallot or small red onion,
    very thinly sliced
Handful potato chips, to garnish

Salma Hage ORIGIN: LEBANON

VEGAN LEBANESE MOUSSAKA
Maghmour

Moussaka is a wonderfully inclusive dish; there are countless different versions of this much-loved recipe. My version is vegan, and maintains the simplicity and richness of flavor that makes this dish so popular. We ate it frequently during my childhood, since feeding a large family meant we rarely ate meat due to its expense. I offer here a modern twist on the traditional Lebanese preparation. A guaranteed crowd-pleaser, it can be served as a main course, or as part of a mezze spread.

Preheat the oven to 400°F (200°C). Line a large baking sheet with parchment paper.

Slice the eggplants into ½ inch (1 cm) disks. Mix the flour, spices, and a pinch of salt and pepper on a large plate. Dab each side of the eggplant slices in the spiced flour mixture to lightly coat. Lay them on the prepared pan, drizzle with the olive oil, and bake for 10 minutes. Flip the pieces over, then bake for an additional 10 minutes, or until browned and cooked through. Remove and set aside to cool, leaving the oven on.

In the meantime, make the tomato sauce: In a large skillet or frying pan, heat the oil over medium heat and sauté the onion for 2 minutes. Add the garlic and cook for 1 minute, then add the cumin and bay leaf and cook for another 1 to 2 minutes. Add the fresh tomatoes, stir, and cook for 3 minutes. Add the sundried tomatoes, tomato paste, canned tomatoes, water, pomegranate molasses, and lemon juice and cook for another 20 to 30 minutes, stirring occasionally, until you have a rich thick sauce. Season with salt and pepper to taste. Turn off the heat and remove the bay leaf.

Layer the eggplant disks in the base of a roasting pan or large casserole dish. Add a layer of tomato sauce, followed by a layer of chickpeas. Repeat until you have used all of your ingredients (about 3 to 4 layers), ideally finishing with a layer of tomato sauce. Return to the oven for 40 minutes. Set aside to cool. This dish is best served at room temperature, when all the flavors are at their best.

Salma Hage is a James Beard Award winner and best-selling author of two Middle Eastern cookbooks. Her cookbook *The Lebanese Kitchen* is considered the definitive book on Lebanese home cooking. Growing up in Mazarat Tiffah (Apple Hamlet), in the mountains of the Kadisha Valley in North Lebanon, she learned to cook from her mother, mother-in-law, and sisters-in-law. Having helped bring up her nine brothers and two sisters, she grew up cooking for the whole family. She has pursued this love for cooking throughout her life, working for many years as a professional cook.

Serves 4

2 large eggplants
¼ cup (1 oz/30 g) all-purpose
  or gluten-free flour
2 teaspoons Lebanese 7-spice
Salt and ground black pepper
2 tablespoons extra virgin olive oil
Two 14 oz (400 g) cans chickpeas,
  drained

TOMATO SAUCE

2 tablespoons extra virgin olive oil
1 onion, finely chopped
4 garlic cloves, finely chopped
1 teaspoon ground cumin
1 bay leaf
2½ lb (1.1 kg) tomatoes (6 large),
  finely chopped
7 sundried tomatoes, preserved in oil
2 tablespoons tomato paste
14 oz (400 g) can diced or chopped
  tomatoes
Scant ½ cup (100 ml) water
1 teaspoon unsweetened pomegranate
  molasses
Juice of ½ a lemon

Pat Tanumihardja ORIGIN: INDONESIA, SINGAPORE

TURMERIC, ZUCCHINI, AND CARROT STIR-FRY
Orak Arik

Most people don't think of summer as prime stir-frying season. It is, in fact, a great time to stir-fry because of the bounty of fresh, tasty vegetables available. One of my favorite childhood dishes is *orak arik*, which in Indonesian refers to any dish scrambled with eggs. My mom used to make it with green beans and carrots. I have chosen zucchini instead, but feel free to roam your farmers' market or grocery store for crookneck squash, okra, or sweet corn! This recipe serves two with rice, but it is typically eaten family-style, alongside other shared dishes.

Swirl the oil into a large wok or nonstick skillet and place over medium-high heat until shimmering hot. Add the garlic and shallots, followed by the turmeric. Stir and cook until the paste is fragrant and darkens in color, 1 to 2 minutes.

Add the carrots and zucchini and toss to coat with the paste. Stir and cook until soft, 2 to 3 minutes.

Slowly pour the eggs over the vegetables and cook undisturbed until they start to set, 45 seconds to 1 minute. Break up the egg into large curds and mix into the vegetables. Sprinkle with salt and pepper, and cook, stirring, until the vegetables are cooked to your liking. Stir in the scallions, and taste and adjust the seasonings, if necessary. Scoop into a serving bowl, top with the cilantro or celery leaves, and serve hot.

Serves 2

2 tablespoons vegetable oil
2 garlic cloves, minced
½ cup (2 oz/60 g) coarsely chopped shallot or red onion
½ teaspoon turmeric
2 medium carrots, peeled and cut into matchsticks
1 medium zucchini, cut into matchsticks
2 large eggs, lightly beaten
½ teaspoon fine sea salt
¼ teaspoon ground black or white pepper
2 scallions, green parts only, chopped
Handful of chopped cilantro or celery leaves, to garnish
Steamed rice, to serve

Born in Indonesia to Indonesian-Chinese parents and raised in Singapore, **Pat Tanumihardja** credits her eclectic culinary aptitude and global outlook to her multicultural background. Pat has been a food and lifestyle writer for over a decade. Her cookbooks include *Farm to Table Asian Secrets: Vegan and Vegetarian Full-Flavored Recipes for Every Season* and *The Asian Grandmothers Cookbook*. She lives in Springfield, Virginia, with her husband and son. Find Pat on Twitter: @PicklesandTea, Instagram: @Pickles.and.Tea, and on the web: SmithsonianAPA.org/PicklesandTea.

Maria Loi ORIGIN: GREECE

BRAISED GIANT BEANS WITH SPINACH

Gigantes me Spanaki

This recipe reminds me of my childhood in Thermo, Greece, growing up on my family's farm, where we grew many types of beans (among other crops). When money was tight, we could always depend on our cache of dried beans to keep us full and nourished. My grandmother knew how to transform beans into many different dishes, sweet or savory, hearty or light. The beauty of cooking with beans is their versatility and affordability—two qualities that are integral to the immigrant experience. The ingredients and method of this recipe are simple, but the resulting dish is complex, rich, and satisfying—and to me, it tastes like home!

Gigante beans are extra-large white runner beans. Look for them in Mediterranean grocery stores, or substitute other white beans. You will need to soak the beans overnight, so plan accordingly.

The night before you plan to serve this dish, place the beans in a large bowl with water to cover by 2 to 3 inches (5 to 8 cm). Set aside to soak overnight. (Soaking the beans overnight reduces the cooking time.)

The following day, drain the beans, discarding the soaking liquid, and place them in a large saucepan. Add enough water to cover the beans by 3 inches (8 cm). Bring to a boil over medium-high heat, and boil gently until tender, 45 minutes to 1 hour. Drain the beans into a large colander.

Preheat the oven to 400°F (200°C).

Preheat a large saucepan over medium heat for 1 minute. Add the onions and sauté until golden and softened, about 7 to 8 minutes. Stir in the cooked beans and olive oil and continue to cook, stirring occasionally, for about 5 minutes. Add the carrots, celery, parsley, dill, garlic, tomato purée, and salt and pepper to taste. Bring to a boil, then remove from the heat.

Transfer the mixture to a medium baking dish. Bake for 30 to 45 minutes, or until the tomato has almost caramelized on top. Remove the baking dish from the oven and stir in the spinach. Set the dish aside for about 5 minutes before serving, to allow the flavors to blend.

Serves 6

2½ cups (1 lb/450 g) dried giant beans (gigantes)
2 medium red onions, finely chopped
¼ cup (60 ml) olive oil
2 medium carrots, peeled and sliced into rounds
1 celery stalk, finely chopped
1 bunch parsley, leaves finely chopped
1 bunch dill, leaves finely chopped
2 garlic cloves, minced
3½ cups (1¾ lb/800 g) fresh or canned tomato purée
Salt and ground black pepper
½–1 lb (225–450 g) baby spinach leaves

Maria Loi is a Greek chef, restaurateur, cookbook author, TV personality, and philanthropist based in New York City, where she runs her acclaimed restaurant, Loi Estiatorio. She was elected global ambassador of Greek gastronomy by the Chef's Club of Greece, and has founded a range of food products, including Loi Pasta, Loi Dips, and soon, Loi Yogurt, sold by Whole Foods Markets in Manhattan. Maria's mission in life is to change the world, one healthy Greek bite at a time!

Carla Capalbo ORIGIN: ITALY

FRITTEDDA

My Sicilian grandparents were bakers, and ran an Italian grocery store in Harrisburg, Pennsylvania, their home after leaving Petralia Sottana in the Madonie Mountains. I didn't visit Sicily until I was in my teens, but all I have to do is see artichokes, peas, and fava beans in the market to want to celebrate the spring with this wonderful dish. It goes so well with the yellow semolina-flour bread that my grandparents made. This dish is very easy to cook but takes time to prepare if you start from whole, just-picked vegetables, so allow for some peaceful time in the kitchen. If you can't find fresh or frozen fava beans, use lima beans.

Squeeze the lemon into a medium bowl of cold water. Prepare the artichokes: Cut off the stem and place this in the acidulated water. Pull off the small leaves around the base of the artichoke and continue snapping off the upper part of the outer leaves until you reach the paler inner leaves. Slice off and discard the upper third section of these paler leaves. Using a small sharp knife, cut away the tough outer skin at the base of the artichoke. Cut the artichoke into quarters. Remove the bristly choke from each quarter and slice each quarter into three even slices. As you finish each segment, drop the slices in the lemon water. Peel the stem and slice it thinly. Repeat with each artichoke.

If your shelled fava beans have a tough outer skin on them, bring a small pan of water to a boil and blanch the beans for 2 minutes. Cool under running water. Peel the outer skin from the beans.

Slice the scallions into 2 inch (5 cm) lengths, and set the white and green lengths aside separately.

Cut the asparagus into 2 inch (5 cm) lengths and set the the tips and stems aside separately.

In a medium saucepan, heat the oil over medium-low heat. Add the potatoes and the white scallion lengths. Cover the pan and cook for 10 minutes, stirring occasionally. Add the artichoke pieces and the green scallion lengths. Cover and cook for 10 minutes more.

Stir in the garlic, asparagus stem lengths, and the measured water. Cover and cook for 5 to 6 minutes.

Stir in the asparagus tips, peas, and fava beans. Season with the salt, and some pepper to taste. Cover and cook for 7 to 8 minutes or until the asparagus is tender. Remove the pan from the heat, stir in the sliced mint, and taste for seasoning. Allow to cool to room temperature before serving, garnished with a few sprigs of fresh mint.

Serves 6

1 lemon
1¾ lb (800 g) artichokes (about
  6 medium)
2 cups (8 oz/225 g) shelled fava beans
  (from about 1¾ lb/800 g pods)
2 cups (8½ oz/240 g) shelled peas
  (from about 1lb 2 oz/500 g pods)
12 oz (350 g) thick scallions, roots cut off
  and outer skin removed
14 oz (400 g) asparagus, woody ends
  cut off
¼ cup (60 ml) extra virgin olive oil
9 oz (250 g) baby potatoes, halved if
  larger than 2 inches (5 cm)
2 young garlic cloves, thinly sliced
1½ cups (350 ml) water
½ teaspoon salt
1 teaspoon finely sliced mint leaves
Ground black pepper
Mint sprigs, to serve

Carla Capalbo is a freelance journalist, photographer, and author of fourteen books on food and wine. Her latest book *Tasting Georgia: A Food and Wine Journey in the Caucasus* was published in 2017. *Collio: Fine Wines and Foods from Italy's Northeast* won a prestigious André Simon Award; and her photography has won several awards, including from the IACP's Culinary Trust. She is closely linked to Slow Food, and a member of the Guild of Food Writers and Circle of Wine Writers.

Didem Hosgel ORIGIN: TURKEY

KURUS WITH SPOON SALAD

I grew up in Southern Turkey in the city of Adana. My mother made this dish a lot for my brother and me because it was inexpensive, easy to prepare and, most importantly, delicious! We eat a lot of bulgur in this region of Turkey, so we're always searching for different ways to use it. *Kurus* is a very versatile dish, delicious served with yogurt and salad, and it makes a great sandwich. Look for pomegranate molasses in Middle Eastern or specialty stores, or substitute lemon juice if you can't find it.

In a mixing bowl, combine the bulgur and the hot water. Mix well, and then cover with plastic wrap and set aside until the water has been absorbed, about 20 minutes.

In a medium pot, cover the potatoes with cold water and season with salt. Bring to a boil, reduce the heat to medium, and cook until tender, about 20 to 25 minutes. Drain the potatoes, grate them or pass through a food mill, and then allow to cool at room temperature.

Line a sheet pan with parchment paper. In a large mixing bowl, combine the plump bulgur, potatoes, Aleppo pepper, cumin, olive oil, flour, egg, and 1 tablespoon salt. Mix until thoroughly incorporated.

Divide the mixture into 20 pieces and form into 3 inch (8 cm) patties using the palm of your hand. Arrange on the sheet pan and refrigerate for at least 30 minutes, or up to 3 days.

Meanwhile, make the spoon salad: in a medium mixing bowl, combine all of the ingredients, tasting the salad before you add the salt.

When you are ready to cook the patties, place a large skillet over medium-high heat and add enough vegetable oil to cover the base by 2 inches (5 cm). Once the oil is hot (about 350°F/ 180°C), place the patties in the skillet and fry until golden brown and crispy, about 3 to 4 minutes per side. Transfer the cooked patties to a plate lined with paper towels and season with salt. Arrange the patties on a serving platter and top with the spoon salad.

Serves 6

1 cup (6 oz/170 g) fine bulgur (size 1)
¾ cup (180 ml) hot water
Salt
1½ lb (700 g) russet potatoes, peeled
1 tablespoon Aleppo pepper flakes (optional)
1 teaspoon ground cumin
2 tablespoons extra virgin olive oil
2 tablespoons all-purpose flour
1 egg
Vegetable oil, for shallow frying

TURKISH SPOON SALAD

1 large tomato, finely diced
1-2 Persian or Lebanese cucumbers, finely diced
½ medium red onion, finely diced
½ cup (1 oz/30 g) chopped mint
½ cup (1 oz/30 g) chopped parsley
2 tablespoons pomegranate molasses
¼ cup (60 ml) extra virgin olive oil
1 teaspoon salt, or to taste

Didem Hosgel was raised in a traditional Turkish family where cooking from scratch and preparing food for family members was an ongoing and cherished practice. After moving to the US in 2001, Didem set her roots in Boston and began working for Chef Ana Sortun at the famed Oleana Restaurant in Cambridge, Massachusetts. After many years at Oleana, she became chef de cuisine at Sofra Bakery, a Middle Eastern-inspired bakery and cafe. At Sofra, she creates innovative new dishes using fresh, local ingredients, while still honoring her Turkish roots.

Brenda Abdelall ORIGIN: EGYPT

KUSHARI

Kushari is a simple, yet hearty vegetarian dish that is popular on the streets of Egypt. It is often considered poor man's food because it is cheap and filling. The dish showcases the simple flavors of Egypt, making it popular among children and world travelers alike, and I always ask for it as soon as my plane lands in Egypt. The red sauce can make or break your *kushari* experience, yet every Egyptian makes it differently. The sauce is a delicate combination of tomato sauce, cumin, chili, and garlic. Some will add vinegar, while others will let the fiery chili dominate.

The dish became part of the national resistance in Egypt during the uprising in 2011. The famous shops that dot the streets surrounding Tahrir Square began to share bowls of *kushari* to help sustain and fill the stomachs of the millions of Egyptians who had taken to the streets.

Pat the onions dry with paper towels. Toss them in the cornstarch and set aside.

In a medium pot, combine the lentils with 1½ cups (350 ml) water. Bring to a boil over medium heat, add 1 teaspoon salt, cover the pot, and reduce the heat to low. Simmer until the lentils are tender, 10 to 15 minutes, adding up to ¼ cup (60 ml) more water if they dry out.

In a separate medium pot, cook the rice: Bring 1½ cups (350 ml) water to a boil over high heat. Once boiled, add the rice, cumin, and 1 teaspoon salt. Reduce the heat to low and simmer, covered, until the rice is tender, about 20 minutes.

Cook the pasta according to the package instructions. Once cooked, drain, rinse with cold water, and set aside.

In a large sauté pan, heat the olive oil over medium heat. Fry the onions until they are light brown and crisp, about 10 minutes (you may need to do this in batches to avoid crowding the pan).

In a separate saucepan, make the sauce: Heat the olive oil. Add the garlic, cumin, salt, and cayenne pepper, if using, followed by the vinegar. Once you smell a rich aroma, add the tomato sauce, and bring to a boil. Reduce the heat to a slow simmer and cook until it thickens slightly, about 10 minutes. If you prefer a thinner sauce, you may wish to mix in up to ¼ cup (60 ml) water.

To serve, place the pasta on a dish. Top with the rice, then the lentils, and then the onions. Serve the warm sauce on the side.

Serves 4

2 large yellow onions, thinly sliced
¼ cup (1 oz/30 g) cornstarch
1 cup (7 oz/200 g) brown lentils
Salt
1 cup (7 oz/200 g) white rice
1 teaspoon cumin
2 cups (6 oz/170 g) elbow macaroni or ditalini
¼ cup (60 ml) extra virgin olive oil, plus more if needed

SAUCE

1 tablespoon extra virgin olive oil
6 small garlic cloves, minced
1 teaspoon cumin
1 teaspoon salt
¼ teaspoon cayenne pepper (optional)
2 tablespoons white vinegar
15 oz (425 g) can tomato sauce

Brenda Abdelall is an Egyptian-American, born and raised in the culturally diverse city of Ann Arbor, Michigan. Her love for Egyptian food grew each summer during her childhood visits to Egypt, which included visits to Alexandrian coastal cities, rural villages, and the growing metropolis of Al Mansoura. After watching her grandmother bake fresh bread, and her aunts roll grape leaves with perfection, Brenda has found the kitchen to be her creative outlet. She runs an award-winning Middle Eastern food blog, midEATS, and teaches Middle Eastern cooking classes in Northern Virginia.

Najmieh Batmanglij ORIGIN: IRAN
POMEGRANATE AND WALNUT KHORESH
Khoresh-e Fesenjan

Coming to America as an immigrant in 1983, it struck me that not only were restaurants from various cultures becoming prevalent, but many ethnic ingredients, and the chefs who knew how to use them, were an important part of the culinary landscape. As an immigrant chef, I am delighted to be able to contribute to a better understanding of Persian food and culture. I contribute this recipe to the many others in this book, which through peaceful communication make America great.

Khoresh is a braise—a more delicate, refined version of a stew. This one from the Caspian region of Iran, traditionally made with duck, is a favorite both inside and outside the country. However, this dish is equally delicious—and nutritious—made without meat, which is what I am giving you here. It is best served with rice or quinoa.

Preheat oven to 400°F (200°C). Line a rimmed sheet pan with parchment paper. Toss the butternut squash cubes with the salt, pepper, and olive oil in the pan, and spread evenly. Roast until tender, about 15 minutes. Set aside.

Make the walnut sauce: In a medium-size Dutch oven or heavy pot, heat the olive oil over medium heat. Add the onions and sauté until golden brown, 10 to 15 minutes. Add the salt, pepper, spices, and walnuts, and sauté for 1 minute.

Transfer the onion-walnut mixture to the food processor. Add the fresh herbs and finely grind. Add 1 cup (240 ml) of the pomegranate juice, and the orange zest, pomegranate molasses, and grape molasses. Mix well to create a smooth, creamy sauce.

Return the sauce to the pot. Add the remaining 3 cups (700 ml) pomegranate juice and half of the roasted squash, and bring to a boil. Reduce the heat to low, cover the pot, and simmer for 45 minutes, stirring occasionally with a wooden spoon to prevent the walnuts from burning.

Taste the khoresh and adjust the seasoning to your liking. It should be sweet and sour: if it is too sweet, add extra pomegranate molasses; if it is too sour, add a little more grape molasses.

Garnish with the remaining butternut squash, and the pomegranate seeds and cilantro sprigs. Serve hot. *Nush-e joon!*

Hailed as "the guru of Persian cuisine" by the *Washington Post*, **Najmieh Batmanglij** has spent the past 37 years cooking, traveling, teaching, and adapting authentic Persian recipes to tastes and techniques in the US. She is author of four award-winning cookbooks, most recently *Joon: Persian Cooking Made Simple*. Her seminal cookbook, *Food of Life: Ancient Persian and Modern Iranian Cooking and Ceremonies*, was called "the definitive book on Iranian cooking" by the *Los Angeles Times*. Najmieh is a member of Les Dames d'Escoffier and lives in Washington, DC.

Serves 4

3 lb (1.4 kg) butternut squash (1 large),
  peeled and cut into ½ in (1 cm) cubes
½ teaspoon salt
½ teaspoon ground pepper
1 tablespoon olive oil
1 cup (5½ oz/150 g) pomegranate
  seeds (1 pomegranate), to garnish
Cilantro sprigs, to garnish

WALNUT SAUCE
2 tablespoons olive oil
2 medium onions, peeled and sliced
1 teaspoon sea salt
½ teaspoon ground black pepper
½ teaspoon turmeric
½ teaspoon ground cinnamon
1 tablespoon ground cardamom
2 teaspoons ground cumin
3 cups (10 oz/280 g) walnut halves
2 cups (4½ oz/125 g) chopped parsley
2 cups (4½ oz/125 g) chopped cilantro
2 cups (4½ oz/125 g) chopped mint
4 cups (1 liter) fresh pomegranate juice
Zest of 1 orange
1 teaspoon pomegranate molasses,
  plus more to taste
1 teaspoon grape molasses, plus
  more to taste

FISH

Ziggy Marley ORIGIN: JAMAICA

COCONUT DREAM FISH

This is one of my favorite creations. We have been cooking with coconut for a long time in Jamaica. You'd get it from the people in the market who would boil it; it wasn't something you would buy in a store. The Coconut Dream Fish is a take on the traditional Jamaican brown stew fish. You fry the sea bass lightly with coconut oil; then cook it down with onion, garlic, and other seasoning. Real herbs and spices from the earth give the best flavor. And then you add the coconut milk, so the whole thing has this deep coconutiness. When I first made it I thought, oh, this is like a coconut dream! Makes you go to bed real nice.

Place the fish fillets in the skillet you plan to cook them in and season them with salt and the lemon pepper. Rub 1 tablespoon of the coconut oil into the seasoned fish, massaging for a few minutes. You've reached stage one of coconutiness. Remove the fillets from the pan and set aside.

Heat the remaining coconut oil in the skillet over medium heat until hot. Return the fillets to the pan and fry for 3 to 5 minutes on each side, until slightly browned. Transfer the fillets to a dish, leaving the skillet on the stove. You've reached stage two of coconutiness.

Add ¼ cup (60 ml) of the vegetable stock to the skillet and scrape all the fish goodness from the bottom, deglazing the skillet and stirring. Lower the heat if necessary, so as to not burn.

Add the onion, bell pepper, garlic, ginger, thyme, allspice, cayenne pepper, and curry powder, and stir until mixture starts bubbling (about a minute or so).

Stir in the coconut milk and the remaining ¼ cup (60 ml) vegetable stock, bring to a boil, then reduce the heat to a simmer.

Gently lay the fish fillets back in the pan and simmer for a few minutes, just so the fish can take on the flavors of the sauce. Try to make sure the fillets are kept whole.

Turn off the heat, transfer to a platter, garnish with the thyme and lime wedges, and serve family style. You've reached the final stage of coconutiness.

Serves 4

4 wild sea bass fillets (about 3 oz/ 85 g each)
Salt
½ teaspoon lemon pepper
4–6 tablespoons coconut oil
½ cup (120 ml) vegetable stock
1 medium onion, sliced
2 medium bell peppers, sliced
3 whole garlic cloves
1 teaspoon grated fresh ginger
2–3 thyme sprigs
6 whole Jamaican allspice berries
½ teaspoon cayenne pepper
½ teaspoon curry powder
½ cup (120 ml) coconut milk
Chopped thyme, to serve
1 lime, quartered, to serve

A seven-time Grammy winner, Emmy winner, humanitarian, singer, songwriter, and producer, **Ziggy Marley** has released twelve albums to much critical acclaim. His early immersion in music came at age ten when he sat in on recording sessions with his father, Bob Marley. Ziggy also recently released his debut children's book *I Love You Too*, a multicultural picture book based on one of Ziggy's most beloved songs of the same title from his Grammy Award–winning album *Family Time*. His latest book is the *Ziggy Marley and Family Cookbook*. He is originally from Jamaica and lives in California.

Mei Chau   ORIGIN: MALAYSIA

TURMERIC SHRIMP WITH CURRY LEAVES

I learned most of my basic culinary skills in my mother's kitchen. She taught me everything—from raising livestock and preparing the animals for slaughter, through the chopping block, and ending at the dining table. This dish reflects the multicultural environment of my upbringing; it combines local ingredients and my Chinese heritage wok cooking. It was invented a year after I moved to New York City, with the help of my large Asian pantry, especially curry leaves, whose smell reminds me of my innocent and unbound childhood. If you can't find curry leaves, substitute chopped fresh dill. You can also use dried chilies instead of fresh: just soak in warm water for 10 minutes before slicing. Serve with rice.

Butterfly the shrimp shells: Using a sharp knife, cut along the curve of the backs, from the head to the tail, cutting about halfway through the shrimp. Remove the veins.

Combine the curry leaves, chilies, turmeric, and pepper and use this to coat the shrimp.

Heat the vegetable oil in a wok or sauté pan over high heat. Cook the garlic and shallots until browned, about 30 seconds.

Lower the heat to medium, add the shrimp, and cook until they turn pink and curl up, about 2 minutes. Turn off the heat, season with the sugar and salt, and serve immediately.

Mei Chau was born into a large Chinese family in Malaysia, which is known for its colorful, mixed culture, dating back to the time when the first West-East trade began. She is the tenth child in her family and grew up in a small fishing village famous for its stretch of white sandy beaches, and for being the home of the giant turtle. She opened her first restaurant, Franklin Station Café, a French/Malaysian bistro in New York City's Tribeca neighborhood, in 1993. Her second restaurant, Aux Epices, was opened in 2013 in Chinatown.

Serves 4

1 lb (450 g) jumbo shrimp with shells
9 fresh or dried curry leaves, cut
  into strips
2 red chili peppers, cut into strips
¼ teaspoon turmeric
⅛ teaspoon ground black pepper
2 tablespoons vegetable oil
3 garlic cloves, chopped
1 tablespoon chopped shallots
½ teaspoon brown sugar
½ teaspoon salt, or to taste

Cara Stadler ORIGIN: CHINA

STEAMED BASS WITH UMEBOSHI SOY SAUCE

I discovered this dish on a visit to Thailand with my partner. They often cook and serve fish whole in Thailand and throughout Asia in general. It creates a much better product, both in flavor and texture, and I love that this is just how things are done in most Asian countries. It also allows you to eat the cheeks of the fish, which are one of my favorite parts!

You can use other whole fish, such as sea bass or branzino in this recipe, but make sure to look for a fish short enough to fit comfortably in your steamer (if you find your fish is too big, you can use a lidded roaster with a rack). Find umeboshi plums and Thai soy sauce in Asian grocery stores. You can easily double this recipe if desired.

Using a food processor or blender, purée the soy sauce and umeboshi plums. Lightly season the fish with salt, place in a bowl, and coat with the plum mixture. Cover and refrigerate for 1 hour to marinate.

In a small bowl, mix the ginger, carrots, snow peas, mushrooms, garlic, fennel, chili pepper, fennel seeds, and coriander seeds.

Once the fish has marinated, prepare your steamer: Pour water to a depth of about 1 inch (2 cm) into the base of a large pot or steamer, and place a steaming rack in it, making sure the water does not rise above the bottom of the rack. Bring to a boil over high heat, then cover and reduce the heat to medium.

Place the fish in a heatsafe bowl or dish that will comfortably fit inside your steamer. Top the fish with the vegetables, and place the dish in your steamer. Steam, covered, for about 20 minutes, or until cooked to your liking. The excess steam will collect in the dish, resulting in a delicious broth. Garnish with cilantro leaves, if desired, and serve immediately.

Cara Stadler is the chef and owner of Tao Yuan Restaurant and Bao Bao Dumpling House in Brunswick and Portland, Maine. Her cooking earned her a James Beard Award nomination in the category of Rising Star Chef, and *Food & Wine* named her Best New Chef in 2014. She is from Harvard, Massachusetts, and has lived in Paris, Philadelphia, Berkeley, Shanghai, Singapore, and Beijing. Her food is the culmination of her heritage and travels.

Serves 2

2 tablespoons Thai soy sauce
2 umeboshi plums (Japanese pickled salt plums), pitted and coarsely chopped, or 1 tablespoon paste
1½ lb (700 g) whole flaky white fish, such as black bass, seabass, or branzino, scaled and gutted
Salt
1 tablespoon finely sliced ginger
1 small carrot, peeled and finely sliced
6 snow peas, finely sliced
4 shiitake mushrooms, sliced
1 garlic clove, finely sliced
1 tablespoon finely sliced fennel
½ serrano chili pepper, finely sliced
1 teaspoon fennel seeds, toasted
1 teaspoon coriander seeds, toasted
Cilantro leaves, to garnish (optional)

Ana Sortun ORIGIN: NORWAY

LEFSE, COD, AND PEAS

My grandfather, Henrik Sortun, emigrated from Norway with his parents and ten siblings when he was 12 years old. I was named for his mother Oleanne (my restaurant Oleana has a slightly different spelling). My great-aunts, his sisters, all have fantastic Norwegian names like Solveig, Heiberg, Auslaug, Tordoss, Hulda, Kjellog, and Sonia.

 Every Christmas eve, my Norwegian family gathers for a meal, and I've only missed one in 49 years. At least **75** people take part, but over the years and extended generations, there can be up to 100 people. Picnic tables are set up in every room—bedrooms, the laundry room, the study, the TV room... Every square inch of the house is occupied. We sit to a dinner of lutefisk and *lefse*. *Lefse* is an unleavened flatbread made from potato that is soft, subtle, and airy. The die-hards like the lutefisk (a fish jelly of sorts), and we have boiled cod to appeal to the masses.

The magic of this dish is in the assembly. You slather a fresh homemade *lefse* with butter and fork-mashed potato, top it with peas and cod, and fold it or roll it up like a burrito. My recipe is inspired by our tradition and refined for a smaller crowd.

Place the potatoes in a large saucepot with enough water to cover the potatoes by 2 inches (5 cm). Bring to a boil over medium-high heat and cook until they are very tender when pierced with a fork, about 20 minutes. Drain and set aside, allowing them to dry out and release all their steam, 3 to 5 minutes.

Put the potatoes through a ricer or food mill. Working quickly, while the potatoes are still hot, add 3 tablespoons (1½ oz/40 g) of the butter, and the salt and cream or milk, and stir everything until you have a thick mashed potato. Divide the mixture in half as equally as possible. Refrigerate one-half of the mixture until it is cool, about 30 minutes (this will be for the lefse). To the remaining potatoes, add the chives or scallions and parsley and season with salt and pepper to taste. Cover with plastic wrap and set aside.

Preheat the oven to 325°F (160°C). When the potato mixture for the lefse is cool, gradually mix in the flour and knead the mixture until you have dough. Turn it out onto a lightly floured surface and gently continue kneading it until it comes together and is smooth. Cut the dough in half and divide each half into 6 pieces, so that you have 12. Roll the pieces into neat little balls so that your edges will be smooth when you roll out the lefse. Cover them with plastic so they don't dry out as you work with them.

Serves 6

3¼ lb (1.5 kg) baking potatoes (4 large), peeled and cut into 2 inch (5 cm) chunks

7 tablespoons (3½ oz/100 g) butter

1½ teaspoons salt, plus more to taste

½ cup (120 ml) heavy cream or whole milk

1 tablespoon chopped chives or finely chopped scallions

1 tablespoon finely chopped parsley

Ground black pepper

1½ cups (7 oz/200 g) all-purpose flour, plus more for rolling

2 tablespoons lemon juice

1½ lb (700 g) boneless, skinless cod fillet

1½ cups (5 oz/140 g) frozen peas

Preheat a heavy cast-iron pan over medium-low heat for 4 to 5 minutes.

On a lightly floured surface, roll one piece of the dough into a long oval. Turn it over and roll it out into a thin round, similar to the thickness of a tortilla (or even thinner if you can). Don't press too hard with the rolling pin because this dough is delicate—it sticks easily and can tear if you aren't gentle enough.

Draping it over the rolling pin, or using a large spatula, place it in the hot pan. Cook just until you see bubbles forming, 2 to 3 minutes. Using a spatula, turn the flatbread over and cook until you see bubbles forming again, about 1 minute. Repeat with the rest of the dough, stacking the finished flatbreads in a sealable plastic bag to lightly steam (alternatively, stack them on a plate, covered with a clean cloth to prevent them drying out). Set aside at room temperature until you are ready to serve.

Melt 3 tablespoons (1½ oz/40 g) of the butter and mix with the lemon juice in a small bowl. Place ¼ cup (1 oz/30 g) flour on a plate. Cut the fish into 3 even chunks and roll each piece in the butter mixture, and then in the flour to lightly coat. Season all sides with salt, place on a baking sheet, and drizzle with any remaining lemon-butter mixture. Bake until the cod is cooked through and easily flakes apart, 8 to 15 minutes, depending on the thickness of the fillet. Flake the fish into bite-size chunks and keep warm, covered with foil.

While the fish is baking, cook the peas: Place the peas in a medium saucepan with 1 tablespoon water and the remaining 1 tablespoon (½ oz/15 g) butter. Cook over medium heat until the peas are tender, 2 to 3 minutes. Season with salt and pepper to taste.

When you are ready to serve, assemble your lefse: Place one lefse on your work surface. Place 3 to 4 tablespoons of the mashed potato over one-half of the lefse, spreading it evenly with a fork. Distribute a few flakes of fish over the mashed potato, and scatter with 2 tablespoons of the cooked peas. Fold the lefse over the filling to make a half-moon. Fold it in half again to make a layered triangle.

You can assemble the triangles an hour or so ahead; warm them in the oven or your cast-iron pan before serving. Store leftover lefse in a sealed plastic bag in the refrigerator (you can reheat in a cast-iron pan for 1 minute on each side).

(Pictured on page 97)

Ana Sortun graduated from La Varenne Ecole de Cuisine de Paris and opened her restaurant, Oleana, in 2001, immediately drawing rave reviews from the *New York Times*. She was named Best Chef in the Northeast by the James Beard Foundation in 2005, and went on to open Sofra Bakery and Café. She is the author of *Spice: Flavors of the Eastern Mediterranean* and, most recently, *Soframiz: Vibrant Middle Eastern Recipes from Sofra Bakery and Café* (with Maura Kilpatrick).

Rawia Bishara   ORIGIN: PALESTINE

BAKED FISH KIBBEH
Kibbet Samak

Growing up in Nazareth, we seldom ate red meat on Friday. The cafeteria at my elementary school would frequently serve *mujaddara* (lentil pilaf), which grew monotonous week after week. After school, my cousin Aida would take me to her house where my aunt Um Sami would feed us her delicious fish *kibbeh*. Hers was the only other cooking my mother really respected. And since Um Sami was on a first-name basis with the local fishermen, she always used the freshest catch.

A few summers ago, my family and I were on our annual deep-sea fishing trip to Montauk Point, New York, and as is our custom, we caught an enormous amount of fish. When I was trying to figure out creative ways to use it all, my aunt's recipe came to mind. It is a wonderful dish for a party, and this recipe can be easily doubled. It is best served with *fattoush* (see page 42).

Combine the spices and zest for the seasoning. Divide the mixture in half; half will be for your shell, and half for the stuffing.

Next, make the shell: Place the bulgur in a large bowl and add enough water to cover the bulgur by ¼ inch (6 mm). Set aside until it absorbs the water, about 30 minutes.

Place the onions in the bowl of a food processor and process until very finely chopped. Remove and set aside. Place the grouper in the food processor and process to the consistency of a paste. In a large bowl, combine the onions, fish, and plumped bulgur. Mix in the hot pepper paste, and the spice-zest mixture you set aside for the shell.

Prepare a bowl of ice water. Dipping your hands in the ice water to prevent sticking, knead the mixture between your palms until it becomes dough-like. Cover and refrigerate.

Next, make the stuffing: Sprinkle ¼ teaspoon of the spice mixture onto the fish with a small pinch of salt. Heat the vegetable oil in a large, heavy-bottomed saucepan over high heat. Fry the fish in batches, gently turning occasionally, until lightly browned on all sides, approximately 8 minutes. Transfer the cooked fish to a plate lined with paper towels.

Pour out the vegetable oil. In the same pan, heat the olive oil over medium heat. Sauté the onions and shallots, stirring, until they are translucent and lightly browned, about 15 minutes. Add the cilantro and cook, stirring, for 2 to 3 more minutes. Add the fried fish, molasses, lemon juice, toasted nuts, and the remaining spice mixture. Stir well, remove from the heat, and taste, adding salt, if needed. Allow to to cool to room temperature.

Serves 6 to 8

SEASONING

1 tablespoon salt
1½ tablespoons allspice
1½ teaspoons cumin
1½ teaspoons ground black pepper
¼ teaspoon cinnamon
Pinch nutmeg
¾ teaspoon dried marjoram
Zest of ½ lemon
Zest of ½ lime
Zest of ½ orange

SHELL

1½ cups (8 oz/225 g) extra-fine bulgur
   (size 0)
½ small white onion, coarsely chopped
1½ lb (700 g) skinless grouper fillet or
   other firm white fish, cut into chunks
1 tablespoon hot pepper paste
   (optional)

(Continued on next page)

Preheat the oven to 350°F (180°C). Coat a 13 inch by 9 inch (33 cm by 23 cm) glass or ceramic oven dish with 1 to 2 tablespoons olive oil. Remove the shell from the refrigerator and divide into halves. Use one batch to evenly line the bottom and sides of the baking dish. Evenly spread the stuffing on top of the shell. Spread the remaining shell paste over the top, pressing it with cold damp hands to level and seal the edges. Use a knife to score just the top layer into portions. Additional designs can be carved into each portion (usually rectangles or triangles).

Bake until cooked through and golden brown, 30 to 40 minutes. Remove from the oven and let cool for 15 minutes before serving, so the portions hold their shape. Garnish with chopped cilantro and almonds, if desired.

(Pictured on page 101)

Rawia Bishara is chef and co-owner of Tanoreen restaurant in Bay Ridge, Brooklyn. She emigrated from her hometown of Nazareth to New York 40 years ago. She is the author of *Olives, Lemons & Za'atar*, published in 2014. Her second cookbook will be released in 2018.

STUFFING

1½ lb (700 g) skinless striped bass fillet or other flaky white fish, cut into 1 inch (2 cm) pieces
Salt
½ cup (120 ml) vegetable oil
¼ cup (60 ml) olive oil, plus more for oiling
2 medium white onions, diced
2 shallots, diced
½ cup (1 oz/30 g) chopped cilantro, plus more to garnish
1 tablespoon pomegranate or grape molasses or citrus juice
1½ tablespoons lemon juice
½ cup (1¾ oz/50 g) slivered almonds, toasted or fried, plus a few more to garnish
¼ cup (1½ oz/40 g) pine nuts, toasted or fried

John Sugimura ORIGIN: JAPAN

CURED AND SEARED SALMON ON RICE

San Buri Salmon on Gohan

I love cured and seared salmon on rice because it represents my early travels to Japan, when my world as sansei was truly enlightened to this cuisine. The experience moved me to later become a sushi chef, making dishes like my grandmother did in her restaurant in the 1930s. In this recipe, I weave a combination of traditional ingredients and techniques (和食 *washoku*). The salmon loin is degreased when it is cured, and searing heightens the fragrance. It's the dish I am asked to make all the time! It is worth making your own nikiri sauce, but you can substitute Kikkoman Sushi and Sashimi Soy Sauce, if you wish. The dish serves two people as part of a larger meal, but can be doubled, if desired.

Transfer the salmon to a small bowl and evenly sprinkle with iodized salt. Cover and refrigerate for 2½ hours to cure. Rinse under cold water and pat dry.

Make the nikiri sauce: Place the dashi kombu in the base of a small pot. Add the soy sauce, sake, tamari, mirin, and bonito flakes. Heat over low heat until small bubbles begin to form around the edge of the pot, just before the mixture simmers; then remove from the heat and steep for 5 minutes. Strain into a bowl and set aside to cool.

About 30 minutes before you'd like to serve, cook the rice: Place the dashi kombu in the base of a small pot. Add the rice, and 1¼ cups (300 ml) water. Bring to a boil, cover the pot, and reduce the heat to very low. Simmer until the water is absorbed and the rice is soft, 20 minutes.

Combine the salt, sugar, and rice vinegar and mix well until the salt and sugar dissolve. When the rice is cooked, fluff with a fork, and pour in the vinegar mixture, mixing well.

Heat the broiler to high. Divide the nikiri sauce between two bowls.

Remove the salmon from the fridge and cut it into ½ to 1 inch (1 to 2 cm) cubes. Place the fish in a small oven-safe sauté pan and generously brush with the nikiri sauce from one of the bowls. Place under the broiler until lightly charred, 5 to 6 minutes. (The USDA recommends cooking salmon to an internal temperature of 145°F/65°C.)

Divide the rice between serving plates. Pile the radish and purple cabbage next to the rice, and top the rice with the salmon. Arrange the scallions and avocado slices on top, and sprinkle with black sesame seeds. Serve the remaining bowl of nikiri sauce on the side.

John Sugimura is executive chef, concept-brand director, and partner at PinKU Japanese Street Food in Minneapolis, Minnesota. He is a second-generation Japanese-American professionally trained sushi chef, whose life-long love of sushi blossomed during time spent in Osaka and Kyoto, Japan. Eating John's cuisine is like eating in his grandmother's restaurant in the 1930s. It is the ultimate expression of flavors, colors, and cooking methods, coming together in an authentic experience that is one of a kind.

Serves 2

4 oz (115 g) sushi-grade salmon fillets (loin if available), skin and bloodline removed
Iodized salt, for curing

RICE

3 inch (8 cm) square dashi kombu (dried seaweed), wiped with a damp towel
1 cup (200 g) medium-grain rice
1 teaspoon salt
1½ teaspoons sugar
2 tablespoons rice vinegar

NIKIRI SAUCE

2 inch (5 cm) square dashi kombu, wiped with a damp towel
2 tablespoons Japanese soy sauce
1 teaspoon sake
1 teaspoon tamari
1 teaspoon mirin
Pinch Japanese bonito flakes

TO SERVE

1 daikon radish, peeled and finely shredded
Small handful thinly sliced purple cabbage
1-2 thick scallions, sliced diagonally
½ avocado, sliced
Pinch Japanese black sesame seeds

STEAMED FISH WITH GINGER-WINE SAUCE

I selected this recipe because it brings back memories of growing up in China. In the morning hours, my mother and I would go to the local seafood market and select the fish for that evening's meal. We had no refrigeration, so freshness was always important. Chinese immigrants to the US carried on this tradition of freshness; that's why you see large tanks of live seafood in many of the Chinese restaurants. Also, steaming was my mother's favorite cooking technique, and for this recipe, steaming preserves the delicate flavor and texture of the fish.

Combine the sauce ingredients in a small saucepan and set aside.

Lightly season the fish with salt and pepper and arrange the pieces on a heatproof dish that fits comfortably in your wok, steamer, or large pot. Top with the ginger and set aside.

Place a steam rack in your wok or pot. Pour water to just below the level of rack and bring to a boil over medium heat. Place the dish containing the fish on the rack. Cover the pot, and steam until the center of fish is opaque, about 6 minutes, adding additional water, if needed. Remove the dish from the rack and pour off the liquid from the dish.

Place the saucepan containing the sauce over medium-high heat. Add the cornstarch solution and cook, stirring, until the sauce boils and thickens, about 3 minutes.

Arrange the fish on a serving plate. Pour the sauce over the fish and garnish with the scallions.

Beloved television host, cookbook author, restaurateur, and certified master chef **Martin Yan** has dedicated his life to promoting Chinese cuisine. Born in Guangzhou in Southern China, Martin was first inspired by his mother in the tiny kitchen of their family restaurant. Since 1982, he has hosted the hugely popular PBS cooking show, *Yan Can Cook*, which has been broadcast in 50 countries and has won numerous awards. He is also host of *Martin Yan, Quick & Easy*; *Martin Yan's Chinatowns*; and *Martin Yan's Hidden China*. He has written more than two dozen cookbooks, owns three restaurants, and has appeared as a guest judge on *Iron Chef America*, *Top Chef*, and *Hell's Kitchen*. He lives in California.

Serves 4

1 lb (450 g) firm white fish fillets, such as red snapper or cod, about ¾ inch (18 mm) thick, cut into serving-size pieces
Salt and white pepper
1 tablespoon slivered fresh ginger
1 teaspoon cornstarch dissolved in 2 teaspoons water
Finely sliced scallions, to garnish

SAUCE

¼ cup (60 ml) Chinese rice wine or dry sherry
3 tablespoons chicken broth
1 tablespoon soy sauce
2 teaspoons vegetable oil
1 teaspoon sugar
Pinch of white pepper

Zareen Khan ORIGIN: PAKISTAN

MUGHLAI FISH CURRY
Machli ka Salan

There is fish curry, and then there is fish curry made by a Memon mom. Luckily, I grew up savoring the latter. *Machli ka salan* was a perennial favorite at our home. The secret lies in choosing the freshest fish money can buy and pairing it with ripe tomato. This dish is traditionally made with whole steaks or fillets, but you can use whatever size pieces you prefer, or even whole fish. It is best enjoyed atop that great canvas for all desi works of culinary art, plain basmati rice.

Heat 2 tablespoons of the oil in a large skillet over medium heat and sauté the onion until translucent and lightly browned, 5 to 7 minutes.

In a food processor or blender, combine the onion, garlic, ginger, coriander, cayenne pepper, turmeric, chili pepper (if using), tomato, yogurt, salt, and ¼ cup (60 ml) water. Process until smooth and set aside. This is your masala paste.

In a large sauté pan, heat the remaining ¼ cup (60 ml) oil over medium heat. Add the cloves and fenugreek seeds and stir. Add the masala paste and cook until the mixture thickens and the oil rises to the top, 10 to 15 minutes.

Add the stock or water, bring to a boil over medium-high heat, lower the heat to simmer, and cook until the sauce consistency is to your liking, 15 to 20 minutes.

Add the fish, and simmer until just cooked, 5 to 10 minutes, depending on the type and thickness of the fish. You may gently turn the fish pieces, if large, but be careful not to break them up too much.

Lower the heat to simmer and gently stir in the dried fenugreek leaves, if using. Simmer until the oil rises to the top, about 5 minutes. Sprinkle with garam masala, and serve with rice.

Zareen Khan is a chef, cooking instructor, and restaurateur of Pakistani heritage. She learned the art of cooking from her mother, aunts, and sister. After teaching cooking classes and launching a successful catering business in the Bay Area, she opened Zareen's Restaurant in Mountain View, California, in 2010, to showcase the foods of Karachi, Bombay, and Punjab. She opened a second location in Palo Alto in 2016. In 2017, Zareen's Mountain View was included in the *Michelin Guide*. Zareen is a member of the Farm-to-Consumer Legal Defense Fund, Weston A. Price Foundation, and Farm Sanctuary.

Serves 4

¼ cup (60 ml), plus 2 tablespoons vegetable oil
1 large onion, chopped
1 teaspoon finely minced garlic
1 teaspoon finely minced ginger
1 tablespoon freshly ground coriander seeds
1 teaspoon cayenne pepper
½ teaspoon turmeric
1 green chili pepper (optional)
1 medium tomato, coarsely chopped
¼ cup (60 g) plain yogurt
1 teaspoon salt, or to taste
4–5 whole cloves
5–6 fenugreek seeds
2 cups (480 ml) fish stock or water
1 lb (450 g) boneless firm white fish fillets or steaks, such as cod or halibut, cut into pieces, if desired
1 teaspoon crushed dried fenugreek leaves (optional)
½ teaspoon garam masala

Anita Jaisinghani ORIGIN: INDIA

KERALA SHRIMP STEW

I love the cooking of Southern India. My mother became quite an expert on it after she emigrated from Sindh to Kerala in 1948, and we enjoyed many a coastal-inspired curry. This one particularly brings a smile to my face because she always cooked her shrimp for about 30 minutes, and I had never eaten succulent shrimp until I arrived in North America! Serve this dish with rice.

In a large sauté pan, heat the coconut oil over medium heat until very hot, but not smoking. Add the mustard seeds, grated coconut, and curry leaves and fry until they pop and sizzle, just a few seconds (keep a cover handy since they can jump!). Add the onion and sauté over medium heat until soft, 10 to 15 minutes.

Add the ginger, zucchini, coriander seeds, chili powder, turmeric, and salt. Cook for 1 to 2 minutes more, stirring frequently. Add the stock or water, and the tamarind paste. Bring it to a boil, cover, and simmer for 2 to 3 minutes, until the zucchini is almost cooked.

Add the shrimp and simmer just until cooked through, about 2 more minutes. Garnish with the cilantro and peppercorns and serve.

Anita Jaisinghani is of Sindhi descent, and was born and raised in Gujarat, India. She came to the US in the 1990s by way of Canada. She owned and operated Indika restaurant in Houston, Texas, for 16 years and is now the chef and owner of Pondicheri, an India-inspired café focusing on street and home cooking with two locations in New York City and Houston, Texas.

Serves 4 to 6

3 tablespoons coconut oil
1 teaspoon mustard seeds
3 tablespoons grated fresh coconut
4 curry leaves (fresh or frozen)
1 large red onion, finely chopped
2 inch (5 cm) piece ginger, grated
1 large zucchini, chopped into 1 inch (2 cm) cubes
1 teaspoon coriander seeds, crushed
2 teaspoons chili powder (such as cayenne)
1 teaspoon turmeric
2 teaspoons salt
½ cup (120 ml) vegetable stock or water
¼ cup tamarind paste
1 lb (450 g) large or jumbo shrimp, peeled and deveined
Chopped cilantro, to garnish
½ teaspoon pink peppercorns, crushed, to garnish

Ejhadji Cisse and Cheikh Cisse ORIGIN: SENEGAL

POISSON YASSA

This is a popular dish from the Casamance region of Senegal, where we grew up. It can be made with either chicken or fish, which is generally marinated and cooked with lots of onions, lemons, and Dijon mustard as the focal point. This recipe is for *poisson* (fish) *yassa*, which brings back memories of warm nights in Senegal, eating this dish with family. It is best served with rice.

Preheat the oven to 425°F (220°C).

In a small bowl, combine the African spice ingredients. Cut several slits in each side of the fish, then rub the garlic and African spice into the fish, placing some of the garlic and a pinch of spice in each slit. Season with salt (pictured at this step).

In a large sauté pan, heat 2 tablespoons of the olive oil over medium-high heat. Add the fish, cook for 2 to 3 minutes per side to brown the skin, and transfer to a large baking pan.

Add the remaining 2 tablespoons olive oil to the sauté pan. Add the onions, peppers, and carrots, and lightly sauté over medium-high heat. After 2 minutes, add the Dijon mustard and vinegar, and cook, stirring, for 2 more minutes. Remove from the heat and toss in the olives, pearl onions, lemon juice, and salt and pepper to taste.

Top the fish with the sautéed vegetables. Transfer the pan to the oven, and bake until the fish is opaque and flakes easily with a fork, about 20 minutes.

Remove from the oven and serve immediately.

(Also pictured on page 219)

Ejhadji Cisse and **Cheikh Cisse** are the owners and executive chefs of Ponty Bistro in New York City. The cousins moved to the United States from Senegal in 1995. They entered the restaurant business fourteen years ago and, between them, have worked for internationally renowned chefs, such as Daniel Boulud at DANIEL, Jean-Georges Vongerichten at Vong and Mercer Kitchen, and others. Ponty Bistro fulfilled their dream to own a restaurant, and features a three-star menu of unique African and French cuisine.

Serves 2 to 4

1¼ lb (570 g) whole branzino or other
  flaky white fish, scaled and gutted
5 small garlic cloves, minced
Salt and ground black pepper
¼ cup (60 ml) extra virgin olive oil
2 medium onions, diced
1 small green bell pepper, diced
1 small red bell pepper, diced
2 medium carrots, peeled and diced
3 tablespoons Dijon mustard
¼ cup (60 ml) white vinegar
4–6 pitted green olives
4–6 pickled pearl onions
Juice of 1 lemon

AFRICAN SPICE

1 teaspoon red pepper flakes
1 teaspoon cayenne pepper
1 teaspoon ground black pepper
1½ teaspoons ground coriander
1½ teaspoons chopped fresh parsley

POULTRY

Mourad Lahlou ORIGIN: MOROCCO

CHICKEN WITH CHARMOULA

Before the development of the poultry industry in Morocco in the 1970s, it was customary to go to the market and pick out a live chicken. The chickens were large and the meat really needed to be soaked and braised or it would be extremely tough. The breed of chicken, *a beldi*, is equivalent to some of the free-range artisan chickens sold in the US. And, this is still what I prefer to use, pure poultry raised by hardworking farmers who take pride in their product. Though it is not as critical in a recipe like this, which marinates the meat in spices and herbs, I still encourage you to seek out the purest ingredients available to you.

Look for preserved lemons in specialty and Middle Eastern grocery stores. The chicken will need to marinate overnight or for at least 6 hours, and you will need 6 long skewers for this recipe (if you use wooden skewers, you will need to soak them for at least 20 minutes).

Stir all of the charmoula ingredients together in a large bowl.

Trim the chicken breasts of any excess fat and remove the tenders. Cut the breasts and tenders into 1½ inch (3 cm) pieces. Add the chicken pieces to the charmoula, turning to coat them, and refrigerate overnight, or for at least 6 hours.

Soak 6 long wooden skewers in cold water to cover for at least 20 minutes (or plan on using metal ones).

Next, make the vinaigrette: Whisk the olive oil, lime juice, and parsley together. Stir in the preserved lemon and set aside.

Preheat a grill to medium-high heat, or heat a large cast-iron grill pan over medium-high heat on your stovetop.

Lift one-quarter of the chicken pieces from the marinade, letting any excess stay in the bowl. Skewer the pieces, leaving about ¼ inch (6 mm) between them, so the chicken will cook evenly. Repeat with the remaining chicken and skewers. Season lightly with salt and pepper.

Lay the skewers on the hot grill or grill pan and don't move until well marked, 2 to 3 minutes. Rotate the skewers 90 degrees and grill to mark with a crosshatch pattern, about 1 minute more. Turn the skewers over and grill until the chicken is cooked through, about 2 minutes.

Carefully remove the chicken from the skewers to a bowl. Add just enough of the vinaigrette to lightly coat the meat, and serve with any remaining vinaigrette on the side.

Serves 4

4 boneless, skinless chicken breasts
   (about 2 lb/1 kg in total)

CHARMOULA

2 tablespoons sweet paprika
2 teaspoons ground cumin
½ teaspoon ground ginger
2 tablespoons coarsely chopped thyme
1 tablespoon coarsely chopped
   flat-leaf parsley
2 teaspoons coarsely chopped cilantro
2 teaspoons finely chopped
   garlic cloves
1 cup (240 ml) extra virgin olive oil
Salt and ground black pepper

VINAIGRETTE

¼ cup plus 2 teaspoons (70 ml) extra
   virgin olive oil
2 teaspoons freshly squeezed lime juice
1½ tablespoons finely chopped
   flat-leaf parsley
2½ tablespoons diced preserved lemon

Arriving in California from Marrakesh in 1985 to study, a homesick **Mourad Lahlou** began to channel his mother and aunts as they prepared traditional Moroccan dishes at home. He started to cook for himself, then for friends. He completed a master's degree in macroeconomics, but the lure of the kitchen pulled him from his doctorate, and he opened his first restaurant, in San Rafael, California, in 1997. He then opened the modern Aziza, named after his mother, in San Francisco in 2001. In 2009, he won *Iron Chef America* by the largest margin in the history of the show. And in 2010, Aziza became the first Moroccan restaurant to receive a Michelin star. He is the author of *Mourad: New Moroccan*.

David SooHoo ORIGIN: CHINA

MUSHROOM AND CHICKEN CHOP SUEY
Moo Goo Gai Pan

The largest migration of Chinese pioneers to California's gold rush occurred between 1849 and 1852. Almost to a man (few women made the journey), they were Cantonese, from the province of Guangdong near Hong Kong. They crossed to San Francisco, on the way to the city where the real search for gold began—Sacramento.

After the gold rush came to an end, thousands turned to jobs building the first transcontinental railroad. In the Sacramento River Delta, they built levees to shore up islands of fertile soil. And through gold, rail, and levees, the Chinese brought their kitchens.

My family continued this tradition. In the early 1950s, my dad and uncle opened a tiny Cantonese restaurant in downtown Sacramento. My uncle was a master chef, and I was around 10 when he began to teach me cleaver techniques, how to butcher a chicken in 20 seconds, and the magical properties of an extremely hot wok. Even after I left home to study, I came back to Sacramento to cook.

The most popular dish on our menu was chop suey, a fabled yet misunderstood dish, often thought of as a lowly stir-fry. But stir-fries are infinite, in the same way rags and silk can both be called clothing. Here is an enlightened stir-fry, the popular *moo goo gai pan*, a wok-full of mushrooms and chicken. It is best served with rice.

Make sure all of your ingredients have been cut, sliced, and measured before you heat your wok.

Heat the wok over high heat until very hot. Add the vegetable oil and sauté the chicken until halfway cooked, about 1 minute. Add the onion and continue to stir-fry until the onion edges are lightly browned, about 30 seconds. Add the carrots and bok choy and cook for another 1 minute, until sizzling again.

Add the button and shiitake mushrooms and the chicken stock. Cover with the lid and simmer for 3 minutes.

Remove the lid and add the salt, sugar, pepper, oyster sauce, wine, and sesame oil. Stir the cornstarch mixture with a fork, and add this to the wok to thicken the sauce, stirring a few times. Turn off the heat and transfer to a serving platter.

To garnish, cut the roots off the enoki mushrooms, if using. Holding all the stems together, stick them upright in the middle of the dish, as if the mushrooms were growing like little trees.

Serves 4

2 tablespoons vegetable oil

1 lb (450 g) boneless chicken breast or thighs, sliced

1 medium yellow onion, sliced

2 medium carrots, peeled and sliced

3 cups (5 oz/140 g) sliced bok choy

5 oz (140 g) white button mushrooms (about 8), sliced

5½ oz (150 g) fresh shiitake mushrooms (about 8), sliced

1 cup (240 ml) chicken stock

½ teaspoon salt

2 teaspoons sugar

¼ teaspoon white pepper

¼ cup (60 ml) oyster sauce

2 tablespoons Chinese rice wine or dry sherry

½ teaspoon sesame oil

¼ cup (1 oz/30 g) cornstarch, dissolved in ½ cup (120 ml) water

7 oz (200 g) fresh enoki mushrooms, to garnish (optional)

David SooHoo was born into the restaurant life. His father, newly arrived in Sacramento from Canton, China, opened many old-style Cantonese restaurants. In 1985, Chef SooHoo and his family opened the modern and lavish 5-star restaurant Chinois East-West. He was the first Sacramento chef invited to cook and teach at the James Beard House in New York.

Anita Lo ORIGIN: CHINA

DUCK E-FU NOODLES

I chose this recipe because it reflects the cuisines of my mother and father's families, who were both Chinese, from Malaysia and Shanghai respectively. Though I am classically trained in French cuisine, I still like to draw on influences from my childhood.

E-fu noodles (also known as longevity noodles, yee-fu noodles, or yi mein) are wide, flat egg noodles made from wheat. If you can't find yu choy, you can substitute bok choy or broccolini. You can also replace the roast duck with 2 confit duck legs instead, if desired (you can find this ready-made in gourmet food stores).

Preheat the oven to 350°F (180°C). Season the duck legs with salt and pepper. Place the duck on the rack of a roasting pan, with enough water to cover the base of the pan by ½ inch (1 cm). Roast until the skin is dark brown, and the meat falls easily from the bone, about 1½ hours. Set aside to rest.

Once the duck has cooked, make the noodles: Bring a large pot of water to a boil. Season heavily with salt (until it tastes like the sea), and boil the e-fu noodles until al dente, about 5 minutes. Drain the noodles and transfer to a warm bowl.

Shred the duck meat. In a sauté pan, heat the peanut oil over high heat. Add the garlic and ginger and stir. Add the yu choy, chives, chili pepper, and the duck meat. Season with salt, to taste, and add 3 tablespoons water. Sauté until the greens are cooked through, uniformly dark green, and the water has evaporated.

Add the sautéed vegetable mixture to the bowl with the noodles, and toss in the oyster sauce, soy sauce, sriracha, and sliced scallions. Taste and season with salt and pepper. Serve immediately.

Anita Lo is a first-generation Chinese-American chef and restaurateur, formerly of the highly acclaimed Annisa restaurant in New York City. She is the author of *Cooking without Borders*. Her second cookbook will be published in the fall of 2018.

Serves 4 to 6

1½ lb (700 g) duck legs with skin
Salt and ground black pepper
12 oz (350 g) package dry e-fu noodles
    (longevity noodles)
3 tablespoons peanut oil
1 large garlic clove, finely chopped
½ inch (1 cm) piece of ginger
8 oz (250 g) yu choy (Chinese greens),
    cut into 2 inch (5 cm) lengths
2 oz (60 g) bunch yellow chives or garlic
    chives, trimmed, cut into 2 inch (5 cm)
    lengths
1 long hot red chili pepper, finely sliced
3 tablespoons oyster sauce, or to taste
3 tablespoons soy sauce
1 tablespoon sriracha
2 scallions, green parts, sliced
    diagonally

Zarela Martinez ORIGIN: MEXICO

CHIPOTLE-LIME CHICKEN

We Mexicans love and use the combination of chili and lime on everything, from mango slices to corn on the cob. Years ago in Papantla, Veracruz, I encountered a bright, citrusy marinade of tiny chiltepin chilies and lime juice, used for chicken or fish. I guessed that it would be just as good—or even better—made with chipotles in adobo, and I was right. Chipotle is universally liked, widely available, and easy to work with. You will need to marinate the chicken, preferably overnight, or for at least 2 hours. Serve this dish with rice, quinoa, or other grains.

In a food processor, combine the garlic and salt and pulse to combine. Rub the oregano between your fingers to release the aroma, and add it to the food processor, along with the chipotles and the sauce that clings to them. Process until smooth. Add the lime juice and vinegar, whirl to combine, and let stand.

Season the chicken with salt and pepper and place in a large bowl. Pour in the marinade and turn the chicken to coat on all sides. Refrigerate overnight or for at least 2 hours to marinate.

When you are ready to cook, remove the chicken from the refrigerator. Using a flexible spatula, scrape the marinade off the chicken into the bowl, and reserve.

Choose a heavy lidded saucepan or Dutch oven large enough to hold the chicken pieces without crowding. Heat the oil over medium-high heat until it ripples, add the chicken, and brown for about 3 minutes on each side. When you are ready to cook, transfer the reserved marinade to the pan. Add the water or stock, bring to a boil, lower the heat to a simmer, and cook, covered, for 20 minutes or until the chicken is cooked through.

Serves 4

1 large garlic clove, peeled and crushed
1 teaspoon salt, plus more to season
1 teaspoon dried Mexican oregano
2–3 chipotle peppers in adobo sauce
Juice of 3 large limes
1½ tablespoons cider vinegar or other mild vinegar
6 chicken thighs (2 lb/1 kg), bone-in and skin-on
Ground black pepper
1–2 tablespoons vegetable oil
1 cup (240 ml) chicken stock, preferably homemade

Born in the Sonoran border town of Agua Prieta, **Zarela Martinez** is a renowned cultural interpreter between Mexico and the United States through the medium of food. For 23 years her eponymous restaurant, Zarela, set standards of authenticity among New York Mexican restaurants. A sought-after speaker and consultant, she also wrote the pioneering cookbooks *Food from My Heart*, *The Food and Life of Oaxaca*, and *Zarela's Veracruz*, the last published in conjunction with her public television series *¡Zarela! La Cocina Veracruzana*. Her website www.zarela.com is an invaluable resource for lovers of Mexican food and culture, and her how-to videos on basic Mexican cooking techniques and flavor principles featured on YouTube are fun and informative.

Tsiona Bellete ORIGIN: ETHIOPIA

SPICY ETHIOPIAN CHICKEN STEW
Doro Wot

I selected this recipe because *doro wot* is the national dish of Ethiopia. It brings a lot of childhood memories and is a special dish that everyone enjoys, especially during holidays, weddings, and family gatherings. Cooking this food is the best way to connect to the culture I left behind.

Berbere is a hot Ethiopian spice mixture, which can be purchased ready-made in grocery stores and specialty markets. Different blends have different heat levels, or you can make your own and adjust it to your taste. Serve this dish with yogurt or cottage cheese, and injera, rice, or pita bread.

Place the chicken in a large bowl, cover with water, and add the lemon juice. Set aside for at least 30 minutes.

Heat a large pot over medium heat and add the onions and ¼ cup (60 ml) water. Cook, stirring, for about 1 hour, or until soft, caramelized, and deep brown in color, adding ¼ cup (60 ml) more water at a time as the onions dry out. You will likely need to use 2 cups (480 ml) water in total.

Add the berbere, garlic, and ginger and cook for 30 minutes, stirring frequently and adding ¼ cup (60 ml) water at a time if it dries out (up to 2 cups/480 ml water in total), until you have a deep red color.

Add the oil and tomato paste and cook for another 15 minutes. Drain and add the chicken, mixing to coat it well with the mixture, and simmer for 30 minutes, stirring occasionally.

Add 3 cups (700 ml) of the water or chicken stock, bring to a simmer, cover, reduce the heat to low, and cook until the chicken is very tender, about 30 minutes.

Remove the lid, add the clarified butter, cardamom, and ½ to 1 teaspoon salt, or to taste. Increase the heat to medium and simmer, stirring occasionally and spooning sauce over the chicken, until the liquid has reduced and the sauce has a thick creamy consistency, about 10 minutes (add the remaining 1 cup/240 ml stock or water during cooking to adjust the consistency, if necessary).

Add the eggs and cook for another 5 minutes to heat through. Season with salt to taste. Serve warm.

Serves 6 to 8

3–3½ lb (1.4–1.6 kg) chicken, cut into pieces, or use chicken thighs
Juice of 2 lemons
12 oz (350 g) red onions (3 medium), finely diced
¼ cup (1¼ oz/35 g) berbere spice
1 garlic clove, minced
1½ teaspoons minced ginger
¼ cup (60 ml) vegetable oil
1 tablespoon tomato paste
3–4 cups (700 ml–1 liter) chicken stock or water, or a mixture
3 tablespoons (1½ oz/40 g) Ethiopian spiced butter or ghee
¼ teaspoon ground cardamom
Salt
6 large eggs, soft boiled and peeled
Plain yogurt or cottage cheese, to serve (optional)

Tsiona Bellete left Ethiopia in 1982 to pursue higher education in the US. After 30 years, living, studying to earn a Master's Degree in Pharmaceutical Sciences, and working, she discovered her passion for cooking. Five years ago, she opened Sheba Restaurant in Rockville, Maryland, followed by Tsiona Foods, a small-batch gourmet Ethiopian food company that brings Ethiopian flair to the American market.

Roni Mazumdar ORIGIN: INDIA

CHICKEN DAHIWALA

This recipe comes from my home; my mother used to make it for us during the hot days of summer. Yogurt does wonders for cooling the body and digestion, so we always enjoyed this healthy, hearty, wholesome dish. The origin of the dish is northern Indian, but many mothers across India make this dish with their own spin. Yogurt is popular in the cooking of northern India, while coconut milk is more common in the southern coastal areas. I have used chicken, but this recipe can also be made using fish or vegetables. It is best served with rice.

In a large sauté pan, heat the oil over medium heat. Add the whole masala ingredients and cook until the spices release their fragrance, 30 to 45 seconds. Add the ginger and garlic and fry until golden brown, 2 to 3 minutes. Add the onions and 2 teaspoons salt, and cook, stirring, until the onions turn golden brown, 4 to 5 minutes.

Add the ground masala ingredients and stir for 30 seconds. Add 2 cups (480 ml) water, bring to a boil, then lower the heat to medium-low and simmer until the sauce thickens, 8 to 10 minutes.

Add the chicken, return the heat to medium, and simmer, stirring occasionally, until it is about three-quarters cooked, 10 to 15 minutes. Stir in the tomato paste, and simmer until the chicken has cooked completely, 8 to 10 minutes.

In a small bowl, whisk the yogurt thoroughly. Just before serving, gradually mix the yogurt into the curry, stirring slowly. Cook for an additional 5 minutes or so to heat through, without letting it come to a boil. Taste, add salt, if needed, and remove from the heat.

Sprinkle with the chopped cilantro, and serve.

Roni Mazumdar is a New York–based restaurateur. Growing up in Kolkata, India, food played a central role in his household. In 2011, he opened the Masalawala, which he runs with his father. Its success led Roni to open a second location in 2016, followed shortly by Rahi, a modern Indian restaurant named *Zagat*'s hottest new restaurant in 2017; and recently, Unico, a globally-influenced fast-casual restaurant in Long Island City, named in *New York Magazine*'s "Best New Cheap Eats, 2017," and *Eater*'s "Hottest Restaurants in Queens." He has used his success to benefit his community, establishing a scholarship program in West Bengal, India; as well as working to empower victims of domestic abuse and sex trafficking in New York City; and staffing and training students from LaGuardia Community College's Food Service Management Program.

Serves 4

¼ cup (60 ml) vegetable oil
1 tablespoon ginger paste or finely chopped ginger
1 tablespoon garlic paste or 3 garlic cloves, minced
2 medium onions, thinly sliced
Salt
3 lb (1.4 kg) boneless, skinless chicken thighs
1 tablespoon tomato paste
2 tablespoons plain whole milk yogurt
¼ cup (½ oz/15 g) chopped cilantro leaves

WHOLE MASALA

3 medium bay leaves
½ teaspoon cumin seeds
3 cloves
1 cinnamon stick
4 green cardamom pods, cracked
5 whole black peppercorns

GROUND MASALA

1 teaspoon turmeric
1 teaspoon cumin
1 teaspoon cayenne pepper
1 teaspoon ground coriander
1 teaspoon garam masala

Sheldon Simeon ORIGIN: PHILIPPINES

CHICKEN ADOBO AND MIXED MUSHROOM FRICASSEE

By far my favorite Filipino dish is adobo. I've always enjoyed my Dad's adobo, but he always spoke of the way my grandmother used to make it. He never learned to make it before she passed away, and he has been trying to replicate it for years, but never could figure it out. In November of 2016, I had the opportunity to cook in Baguio City, Philippines. There, I learned to make an adobo from the Ilocos region. When I returned home, I cooked this dish for my father. At first bite his eyes lit up, "This tastes exactly how Grandma made it."

Heat a large nonreactive sauté pan over medium-high heat. Add the oil, and evenly brown the chicken on all sides, about 5 minutes. Add the garlic, soy sauce, vinegar, peppercorns, bay leaves, and 1 cup (240 ml) water. Bring to a boil, then lower the heat and simmer, covered, over low heat for 15 minutes. Turn the chicken pieces over, replace the lid, and continue to simmer for a further 10 minutes.

Remove the lid, increase the heat to high, and return the sauce to a boil. Boil until the sauce has reduced by half, 10 to 15 minutes, basting the chicken occasionally.

Heat a separate sauté pan over high heat. Add the olive oil, followed by the mushrooms, garlic, and thyme. Sauté for 1 minute, or until tender. Add the parsley, and salt and pepper to taste.

Place chicken on a large platter and top with the sauce. Spoon the mushrooms over the top.

Serves 4

2 tablespoons canola oil
8 chicken drumsticks (about 2 lb/1 kg)
8 garlic cloves
¼ cup (60 ml) soy sauce
½ cup (120 ml) apple cider vinegar
1 teaspoon whole black peppercorns
2 bay leaves

MUSHROOMS

2 tablespoons olive oil
1½ cups (3½ oz/100 g) mixed fresh
  mushrooms, such as shiitake, king,
  and shimeji, sliced or cut into bite-
  size pieces
4 garlic cloves, smashed
4 thyme sprigs
2 tablespoons chopped fresh Italian
  parsley
Salt
Ground black pepper

Born in Hilo, Hawaii, **Sheldon Simeon** acquired his love for cooking from his Filipino parents. Trained at the Culinary Institute of the Pacific and Maui Culinary Academy, he competed in the 10th and 14th seasons of Bravo Network's *Top Chef: Seattle* and *Charleston* as a finalist, winning "Fan Favorite" both times. After serving as the executive chef at Maui's Mala Wailea, MiGRANT, and Star Noodle, he was nominated for two James Beard Awards: Rising Star Chef of the Year, and Best New Restaurant, and was named *Food & Wine*'s People's Best New Chef for the Pacific & Northwest in 2014. He is chef and owner of Tin Roof in Kahului, Maui, serving up his playful take on classic local dishes.

Ingrid Hoffmann ORIGIN: COLOMBIA

RICE WITH CHICKEN
Arroz con Pollo

If there is one dish that means home and conjures my childhood, it is *arroz con pollo*. Mom made it once a week; it became a guessing game as I was picked up from school if that day would be the *arroz con pollo* day. Every Latin American country and family has its own versions. You can double up on the veggies and reduce the rice quantity, or use quinoa for variety. I always make big batches and freeze them in portions.

In a large Dutch oven or deep sauté pan, combine the chicken, quartered onion, 1 cup (240 ml) of the chicken broth, the beer, adobo, Worcestershire sauce, half of the cilantro, and the garlic. Bring to a boil over high heat, reduce the heat to medium-low, cover, and simmer until the chicken is cooked through, 30 to 35 minutes. Remove the chicken to a plate and set aside to cool. When it is cool enough to handle, remove the meat from the bones, shred it, and set aside. Strain the cooking liquid into a bowl through a fine-mesh sieve, discarding the solids.

Pour the cooking liquid into a large measuring cup and add enough of the remaining chicken broth to make 4 cups (1 liter). Return the broth to the pot, and add the rice, peas, carrots, green beans, ketchup, and salt. Stir well and bring to a boil over high heat. Let the liquid evaporate to just below the level of the rice, about 10 minutes, and then reduce the heat to low, cover the pot, and cook until the rice is tender and fully cooked, 25 minutes.

Meanwhile, melt the butter in a large skillet over medium heat. Add the bell peppers and the sliced onion half, and cook until tender, about 8 minutes. Add the shredded chicken and the olives to the vegetables. Cook until it is heated through, 2 to 3 minutes. Fluff the rice with a fork and gently stir in the chicken-vegetable mixture. Sprinkle with the remaining cilantro and serve.

Serves 6 to 8

3–4 lb (1.4–1.8 kg) chicken, cut into
   8 pieces, rinsed and patted dry
1 yellow onion, quartered, plus ½ yellow
   onion, thinly sliced
Up to 4 cups (1 liter) low-sodium
   chicken broth
1 cup (240 ml) light beer, such as lager
3 tablespoons Todo Adobo (recipe
   right) or complete adobo seasoning
3 tablespoons Worcestershire sauce
1 cup (2 oz/60 g) chopped cilantro
   leaves
6 garlic cloves, coarsely chopped
3 cups (1¼ lb/560 g) white rice
1 cup (5 oz/140 g) green peas
   (fresh or frozen)
2 medium carrots, peeled and
   finely diced
8 oz (225 g) green beans, trimmed and
   sliced into 1 inch (2 cm) pieces
1 cup (240 ml) good-quality ketchup
1 teaspoon salt
3 tablespoons (1½ oz/40 g) unsalted
   butter
½ red bell pepper, thinly sliced
½ green bell pepper, thinly sliced
1 cup (5½ oz/150 g) pimento-stuffed
   or pitted green olives

TODO ADOBO

Combine all the ingredients in a small glass jar with an airtight lid and shake to blend. Store in a cool, dry place for up to 2 weeks.

(Pictured on page 131)

Colombian-born **Ingrid Hoffmann** developed a love for cooking as a child, learning from her mother, a Cordon Bleu–trained chef. As a teenager, she worked in her mom's catering business. Upon moving to Miami, they opened a restaurant together. As host of *Top Chef Estrellas* on Telemundo, *Delicioso* on Univision, and *Simply Delicioso* on the Cooking Channel, Ingrid has become a leading Latin authority on cooking and lifestyle, and her Delicioso brand has become one of the most recognizable, trusted, and entertaining food brands for Hispanic America. Find her at www.ingridhoffmann.com.

Makes ½ cup (3½ oz/100 g)

1 tablespoon lemon pepper seasoning
1 tablespoon garlic powder
1 tablespoon onion powder or flakes
1 tablespoon dried oregano
1 tablespoon parsley flakes
1 tablespoon achiote powder (annatto seeds)
1½ teaspoons ground cumin
1 tablespoon salt

MEAT

Aarón Sánchez ORIGIN: MEXICO

CARNITAS TACOS

At large gatherings, this dish was a family favorite. During summers in El Paso, we would get everyone together and throw these huge fiestas, and the carnitas tacos were always a big hit. It's a communal dish that is rich and layered in flavor, and some of the best childhood memories I have are of eating this dish with family and loved ones.

In a nonreactive stockpot, combine the brine ingredients with enough water to cover the pork (about 8½ cups/2 liters). Bring to a boil, then remove from the heat and let cool completely. Add the pork to the pot, and refrigerate for at least 12 hours or up to 24 hours.

Once the pork has brined, preheat the oven to 275°F (135°C). Remove the pork from the brine, patting it dry with paper towels, and cut it into 2 inch (5 cm) pieces.

In a large Dutch oven, heat the fat over medium heat until it melts. Add the pork pieces, cover the pot, and roast in the oven until the meat is very tender, about 2 hours. Transfer the meat to a mixing bowl, discarding the oil. Finely chop the chipotles and add them to the meat with their sauce. Add the orange and lime juice, toss to combine, and season with salt and pepper to taste.

To assemble, spread each tortilla with crema, if using, and top with a generous amount of the seasoned pork. Sprinkle with the pickled onions and jalapeños, if using, and top with cucumber slices, cilantro, and a squeeze of fresh lime.

PICKLED RED ONIONS OR JALAPEÑO PEPPERS

Makes about 1 pint (1 lb/450 g)

1-1¼ cups (240-300 ml) white wine vinegar
2 tablespoons sugar
2 tablespoons table salt
1 cup (4 oz/115g) thinly sliced red onion or jalapeño peppers

In a small pot, combine the vinegar, sugar, and salt and bring to a boil, stirring to dissolve. Remove from the heat and cool to room temperature. Place the onion or jalapeño slices in a jar or tub, pour in the vinegar mixture to completely cover them, seal, and refrigerate for at least one hour before using, or for up to several days.

Serves 6 to 8

3½ lb (1.5 kg) boneless pork shoulder
3-4 cups (1⅓-1¾ lb/600-800g)
    rendered pork fat or lard (or more,
    if needed to mostly cover the meat)
Half a 7 oz (200 g) can chipotle peppers,
    in adobo, or more to taste
Juice of 1 orange
Juice of 1 lime
Salt and pepper

BRINE

1 teaspoon coriander seeds
1 teaspoon cumin seeds
1 teaspoon fennel seeds
1 bay leaf
1 stick canella (Mexican cinnamon)
1 cup (7 oz/200 g) brown sugar
1 cup (8 oz/225 g) kosher salt

TO SERVE

18-24 small tortillas
1 cup (240 ml) Mexican crema or sour
    cream (optional)
½ cup (3½ oz/100 g) pickled red onions
½ cup (4 oz/115 g) pickled jalapeño
    peppers (optional)
Cucumber slices, seeds removed
1 bunch cilantro, leaves separated
Lime wedges

Aarón Sánchez is an award-winning Mexican-American chef and TV personality. He is the chef and owner of Johnny Sánchez, with locations in New Orleans and Baltimore, and a judge on FOX's hit culinary competition series *Masterchef*. He co-starred on Food Network's *Chopped* and *Chopped Junior*, and is the author of two cookbooks. An active philanthropist, Aarón launched the Aarón Sánchez Scholarship Fund, enabling aspiring chefs from the Latin-American community to attend culinary school. Aarón is passionate about preserving his family's legacy through food and encouraging diversity in the kitchen.

Cathal Armstrong ORIGIN: IRELAND

IRISH BEEF STEW

On any given day in my Mam and Da's kitchen, until I moved to the United States at twenty years of age, the conversation centered around food. Da was an avid gardener who took pride in cooking with the sixty-plus kinds of fruits and vegetables he grew on our Dublin property on Watson Road. It was extremely rare for the times that a family living in Dublin would have such a garden—and that a man would cook. I've chosen this recipe because it is close to my heart, and reminds me of my Irish background and my parents, who instilled in me the importance of home, culture, family, and locally sourced food.

Brown the beef: Pat the beef cubes dry on all sides with paper towels and season well with salt and pepper. Heat a large sauté pan over medium-high heat for several minutes. Add the canola oil. Distribute the beef evenly across the bottom of the pan without crowding it and try not to disturb the meat for 3 to 4 minutes, then turn the cubes over and brown them on the other side for another 3 to 4 minutes.

Add the onions, carrots, and celery to the pan, stirring them with a flat-edged wooden spatula, until translucent but still firm, 4 to 5 minutes. As the vegetables cook, water will release and deglaze the pan. Use the spatula to scrape any brown bits from the bottom of the pan as you go. Stir in the garlic and cook for 1 minute.

Stir in the flour and allow it to brown lightly for about 2 minutes. Add the broth, scraping up any brown bits from the bottom of the pan. Stir in the chili, bay leaves, rosemary, and thyme. Transfer the stew to a Dutch oven or lidded pot and bring it to a boil over medium-high heat. Lower the heat, cover the pot, and simmer the meat slowly for 2 hours, until it is very tender. Adjust the salt and pepper to taste. Serve hot.

Serves 4 to 6

1½ lb (700 g) stew beef, such as
   shoulder or chuck, cut into
   1 inch (2 cm) cubes
Salt and ground black pepper
1 tablespoon canola oil
1 large yellow onion, diced
4 large carrots, peeled and diced
4 celery stalks, diced
8 garlic cloves, coarsely chopped
2 tablespoons all-purpose flour
5 cups (1.2 liters) beef broth
1 serrano chili pepper, coarsely
   chopped, with seeds
3 large fresh bay leaves
1 tablespoon chopped fresh
   rosemary leaves
2 tablespoons chopped fresh
   thyme leaves

A native of Dublin, Ireland, **Cathal Armstrong** is the chef and owner of Restaurant Eve, the flagship among his chain of Alexandria, Virginia, establishments, where he balances a commitment to locally sourced, fresh ingredients with a fine-dining experience. He has been recognized by the James Beard Foundation with nominations for Best Chef, Mid-Atlantic in 2011, 2012, and 2013. *Food & Wine* included him among their "10 Best New Chefs" in 2006, and their "50 Hall of Fame Best New Chefs." He has also been recognized for his contributions to the local food movement and for his work to preserve and protect the environment. Under President Obama's Winning the Future initiative, the White House honored him as a "Champion of Change." He is author of *My Irish Table: Recipes from the Homeland and Restaurant Eve.*

Cristina Martinez ORIGIN: MEXICO

PORK RIBS WITH PURSLANE
Verdolagas con Costilla de Puerco

This is a special recipe from my mother, Ines. She would cook this dish on Thursdays, because that was the day the purslane arrived from the farm. All of us would help prepare the purslane leaves, because it was a lot of work! The dish is seasonal, and we only eat it for about three months per year. When my mother arrived in America to visit, this was one of the first things I asked her to cook, and we served it here at our restaurant as a *guisado* (stew).

Purlsane grows wild in many parts of the United States. Look for it in farmer's markets or Latin American grocery stores. (You can substitute spinach, though the flavor will be slightly different.)

Place the pork ribs in a large pot with one onion half, 2 garlic cloves, and the salt. Add enough water to cover the meat, and bring to a boil, skimming any foam that forms. Reduce the heat, cover the pot, and simmer until the meat is very tender, 45 minutes. Remove the meat, lightly season with salt, and set aside. Strain and set aside the stock.

In a medium saucepan, bring about 2 cups (480 ml) water to a gentle boil over medium heat. Add the tomatillos and jalapeños, and steam, covered, until they change color, about 10 minutes.

Heat 1 tablespoon of the oil in a comal or cast-iron skillet, and sear the remaining onion and garlic until just charred (this is traditional, but you can skip this step, if preferred). Coarsely chop the onion and garlic.

In the bowl of a food processor or blender, combine the tomatillos, peppers, onion, and garlic and blend to a thin sauce, adding some of the reserved stock to thin it, if necessary. Set aside.

In a medium pot, bring about 2 cups (480 ml) water to a gentle boil over medium heat. Add the purslane leaves and a pinch of salt, turn down the heat, and simmer just until tender, 3 to 5 minutes. Drain.

Heat 1 to 2 tablespoons oil in a large saucepan over high heat, and, working in batches, if necessary, brown the meat, about 2 minutes each side. Add the salsa and purslane and bring to a boil. Lower the heat, cover the pot, and simmer until the liquid thickens to a thin sauce and the dish comes together, about 10 minutes. (If the sauce is too thick for your liking, add a little of the reserved stock.) Season with salt, to taste, and serve with fresh tortillas.

Serves 4

2–3 lb (1–1.4 kg) pork spare ribs,
    cut into 1- or 2-rib pieces
1 small onion, halved
4 garlic cloves
1 tablespoon salt, plus more
    for seasoning
1½ lb (700 g) small tomatillos, husked
2–4 green jalapeño peppers,
    stems cut off
2–3 tablespoons vegetable oil
1½ lb (700 g) purslane, leaves picked
    (5 cups/12 oz/350 g leaves)
Fresh tortillas, to serve

Cristina Martinez crossed the desert to come and make a career in the United States. As an undocumented female chef and restaurateur, she challenges gender stereotypes and raises awareness for the plight of undocumented workers through her restaurant, El Compadre, in Philadelphia, Pennsylvania. In 2016, *Bon Appétit* named her first restaurant, South Philly Barbacoa (now closed), in the top 10 of their "Best New Restaurants in America." Cristina was born into a family of *barbacoieros* in Capulhuac, Mexico, and was raised cooking in the family business. She lives in Philadelphia with her husband, Benjamin.

Ariane Daguin ORIGIN: FRANCE

SPRING RABBIT STEW

The Italians and French eat rabbit the way Americans eat chicken, which is to say, quite often. Rabbit meat is tender, lean, delicious, and as versatile as chicken, to which it can also be compared in taste. This light spring stew is full of flavor from pancetta, tender rabbit, white wine, and a ton of fresh herbs and vegetables. If you can't find hon shimeji mushrooms, use sliced fresh shiitake mushrooms. Serve this dish with crusty bread.

In a large sauté pan, heat the oil over medium-high heat. Season the rabbit with salt and pepper, and brown the meat until golden on all sides, about 5 minutes. Remove from the pan and set aside. Add the ventrèche or pancetta and sauté until browned and crisp. Remove with a slotted spoon (leaving the rendered fat) and set aside on paper towels to drain.

Lower the heat to medium and add the shallot, leek, and garlic; sauté until shallot pieces are translucent and the leek slices have softened. Add the carrot and celery, and sauté for about 3 minutes more. Sprinkle the flour over the vegetables in the pan, stirring to coat, and continue to cook until the flour turns golden, 3 to 5 minutes. Return the pan to medium-high heat.

Stir in the wine, scraping up any browned bits, and cook for about 2 minutes. Stir in chicken stock, and add the bay leaf and thyme sprigs. When mixture comes to a simmer, lower the heat to medium-low and return the rabbit to the pan. Add the mushrooms and potatoes. Cook for 15 minutes, then add the fresh peas (if using frozen, you will add these later). Cover and continue to cook until rabbit is tender and cooked through, about 25 more minutes.

Remove the rabbit pieces and set aside. Discard the bay leaf and thyme stems. Increase the heat to high and reduce the sauce until it thickens. Remove from the heat, stir in the crème fraîche and Dijon mustard, and season to taste with salt and pepper. At this point, you can shred the rabbit meat, discarding the bones, or leave it as it is. Return the rabbit to the sauce, add the peas (if using frozen), and return to medium heat to heat through, if necessary. Top with the parsley and tarragon and serve.

Serves 4

2 tablespoons olive oil
4 rabbit legs (2 lb/1 kg in total)
Salt and ground black pepper
3 oz (85 g) ventrèche or pancetta, diced
1 shallot, diced
1 leek, white and light green parts only, thinly sliced
2 garlic cloves, minced
2 carrots, peeled and diced
1 celery stalk, diced
3 tablespoons all-purpose flour
1 cup (240 ml) dry white wine
2½ cups (600 ml) chicken stock
1 bay leaf
3 fresh thyme sprigs
8 oz (225 g) organic hon shimeji mushrooms, trimmed
12 fingerling potatoes (about 1 lb/ 450 g), halved
1 cup (4 oz/115 g) green peas (fresh or frozen)
½ cup (4 oz/115 g) crème fraîche
1 tablespoon Dijon mustard
1 tablespoon chopped fresh parsley
1 tablespoon chopped fresh tarragon

Recognized as one of the mothers of modern food culture, **Ariane Daguin** is the founder, owner, and CEO of D'Artagnan, the leading purveyor of sustainable, humanely-raised meats, charcuterie, foie gras, and mushrooms in the United States. Since D'Artagnan's founding in 1985, Ariane has emerged as a culinary innovator among America's top chefs, partnering with small family farms dedicated to natural production of the finest quality and healthiest meat, game, and poultry. A pioneer in the farm-to-table movement, Ariane introduced the first organic, free-range chicken years before the USDA allowed the word "organic" on the label. Ariane continues to influence and inspire the food industry by introducing new products, creating new animal breeds, and implementing innovative and ecologically responsible methods of production.

Josh Ku and Trigg Brown ORIGIN: TAIWAN

FLY'S HEAD
Budding Chives with Pork and Fermented Black Beans

My family is from Taiwan. My mother's side is from Southern Taiwan. My father's side came over with Chiang Kai-shek in the 1950s and my dad grew up on a military base in rural Northern Taiwan. So my family had two very different cooking styles, which together represent Taiwan's diverse cuisine. —Josh

We built our relationship around Taiwanese food, and brought our version of the cuisine to Brooklyn with the intention of building bridges and raising awareness of Taiwanese identity. One of the dishes we bonded over originally was Fly's Head. This is my recipe for the Taiwanese dish with Szechuan roots. It's a favorite go-to that represents the multicultural influences and melting-pot nature of food in Taiwan. Of course there are more iconic dishes, but this is a fun recipe that's important to Josh and I—and one that's relatively simple to make at home. —Trigg

Look for chives with unopened buds in Asian grocery stores or farmers' markets in spring and summer, or grow your own. We have provided substitutes where possible, but it is worth making a trip to your local Asian grocery store for this recipe. Serve with steamed rice.

Serves 4

2 tablespoons cornstarch
1¼ lb (560 g) ground pork
¼ cup (60 ml) vegetable oil
Salt
¼ cup (60 ml) shoaxing (Chinese rice wine) or dry sherry
1 cup (240 ml) mirin (Japanese sweet wine) or honey or agave syrup
1 tablespoon hon dashi (bonito stock granules)
3 tablespoons light soy sauce
1½ lb (700 g) budding chives (about 5 bunches), trimmed, cut into ½ inch (1 cm) pieces
4 garlic cloves, grated or minced
4 bird's eye chilies, thinly sliced
3 tablespoons toasted sesame oil
2 tablespoons fermented black beans

Mix the cornstarch with 2 tablespoons water to make a slurry. Velvet the pork by massaging the cornstarch mixture into the meat, along with 1 tablespoon of the vegetable oil and a small pinch of salt. Cover and refrigerate for 30 minutes.

In a large nonstick skillet, heat the remaining 3 tablespoons oil over high heat. Cook the pork, pressing down to encourage browning and stirring occasionally, until almost cooked through, but with some remaining pink spots, about 3 minutes.

Add the shoaxing, mirin, hon dashi, and soy sauce, bring to a simmer, and cook, pressing down firmly on the pork to break it into small pieces, until the liquid has reduced by half and the meat looks slightly glazed, about 3 minutes.

Add the budding chives, garlic, chilies, sesame oil, and fermented black beans. Cook, tossing, until the chives are just tender and very fragrant, about 1 minute. Serve over rice.

Josh Ku and **Trigg Brown** met at a cookout and bonded over Taiwanese food. Eating and cooking Taiwanese food became a regular activity that elucidated the lack of Taiwanese representation in the NYC culinary landscape. Their restaurant, Win Son, in Williamsburg, Brooklyn, communicates their version of Taiwanese food, and raises awareness for the nuanced and complex nature of Taiwanese food, culture, politics, and history.

Moussa Doulaeh   ORIGIN: SOMALIA, DJIBOUTI

AFRO STEAK DINNER

I learned the power of food from my father, who used herbs and spices as medicine to help others. He first taught me the importance of using fresh ingredients and treating them with respect. This dish truly represents Somali and East African culture, using ingredients that can be found here in the US. In Somalia, goat meat is fairly common, while beef is somewhat of a delicacy because of how highly cattle are valued. This dish includes tasty portions of spiced beef with grilled vegetables. Aromatic Somali rice, bursting with sweet and savory flavors, is a natural match. There will be enough rice for leftovers or large appetites, but you can easily halve the recipe, if preferred.

First, make the rice: Heat the oil in a medium saucepan over medium heat. Add the garlic, cinnamon stick, and jalapeño, and sauté for a few seconds, until fragrant. Add the onion and peppers and sauté until the onions are translucent, 3 to 5 minutes. Stir in the curry powder and cumin.

Add the stock or water and the salt and bring to a boil. Add the rice and cilantro, bring back to a boil, then reduce the heat to very low, and cook, covered, until the rice has absorbed the water, about 20 minutes. Turn off the heat and let stand for 5 minutes with the lid on, then fluff with a fork, remove the jalapeño, and mix in the golden raisins, if using.

To make the steak sauté: Heat the vegetable oil in a large sauté pan. Add the garlic, followed by the steak, and sear the meat on both sides for about 30 seconds on each side. Season the meat in the pan with the berbere spice, adobo, and chicken stock powder.

Reduce the heat to medium, add the onions and mixed peppers, and cook until the vegetables have softened and the liquid in the pan has evaporated, about 3 minutes. Add the tomato purée and cilantro and cook until the steak is cooked to your liking and the liquid has reduced to a sauce consistency, 5 to 7 minutes.

Serve the meat atop the rice, garnished with chopped cilantro.

Moussa Doulaeh is executive chef and co-owner of Afro Deli, a fusion restaurant with locations in St. Paul, and Minneapolis, Minnesota. At Afro Deli, he combines the cuisine of his native East Africa, with the many flavors learned from his formal culinary training in top Canadian and American kitchens, or gathered from cooking with friends from around the world. In April 2017, Afro Deli initiated the Dine Out for Somalia campaign, a fundraiser with 50 participating restaurants, to support famine relief efforts.

Serves 4 to 6

RICE

2 tablespoons vegetable oil
2 garlic cloves, minced
1 cinnamon stick
1 jalapeño pepper, whole
½ medium onion, finely chopped
½ small or ¼ large green bell pepper, finely sliced
½ small or ¼ large red bell pepper, finely sliced
½ teaspoon curry powder
1 teaspoon cumin
5 cups (1.2 liters) chicken stock or water, or a combination
1½ teaspoons salt, or to taste
3 cups (1¼ lb/560 g) long-grain white rice
¼ cup (½ oz/15 g) chopped cilantro
1–2 tablespoons golden raisins (optional)

STEAK SAUTÉ

1–2 tablespoons vegetable oil
2 garlic cloves, finely chopped
2 lb (1 kg) sirloin steak, thickly sliced
2 teaspoons berbere spice mix
½ teaspoon Adobo seasoning
1 teaspoon chicken stock powder
1 medium onion, sliced
½ medium green bell pepper, sliced
½ medium red bell pepper, sliced
½ cup (120 ml) puréed tomatoes
1 teaspoon chopped cilantro, plus more to garnish

IMMIGRANT'S BEEF

I joined the Fat family restaurant business in 1974, when my father-in-law, Frank Fat, opened his second restaurant, China Camp, in Old Sacramento. I developed this recipe for its menu, in order to commemorate the Chinese immigrants who came to the US looking for the "gold mountain" during the Gold Rush era, as well as the building of the railroads. This dish is typical of Chinese immigrants; it is cooked with local meats and produce, but flavored with the spices and herbs they brought with them from China. Today, at California Fat's, we've retained the zesty flavor of the dish, but updated the presentation: tender medallions of flank steak are served over fresh seasonal vegetables. We serve this dish with rice.

Trim the fat from the meat. Holding your knife at an angle, cut the steak lengthwise into ¼ inch by 3 inch (6 mm by 8 cm) strips; then cut diagonally, across the grain, to make 2 inch (5 cm) pieces.

In a medium bowl, combine the soy sauce, vegetable oil, brandy, garlic, ginger, sesame oil, and cornstarch. Add the beef and stir to coat. Cover and refrigerate overnight, or for at least 2 hours.

Just before cooking the meat, bring a large saucepan of salted water to a boil. Blanch the asparagus or broccoli until just tender, about 3 minutes. Drain, rinse with cold water, and drain again; arrange on a serving platter.

Heat 2 to 3 teaspoons vegetable oil in a wide heavy frying pan over high heat. Sauté the meat for 1 to 2 minutes on each side, until cooked to your liking. Arrange the meat over the green vegetables and serve immediately.

Born in Hong Kong, **Lina Fat** was a pharmacist in Sacramento, California, for many years, before joining her husband's family's restaurant business in 1974. Her passion for cooking and menu creation landed her the role of head chef when the Fat Family Restaurant Group expanded, with the opening of their second restaurant, China Camp, in 1974, followed by Fat City Bar & Café in 1976. Today, Lina wears several hats in the Fat Family Restaurant Group. She is vice president of culinary research and development, and oversees four restaurants and a catering division. She continues to play an active role in the community, promoting cultural diversity throughout the Sacramento area.

Serves 4

1½–2 lb (700 g–1 kg) flank steak
¼ cup (60 ml) soy sauce
¼ cup (60 ml) vegetable oil, plus
    more for cooking
1 tablespoon brandy
3 small garlic cloves, minced
1 tablespoon minced fresh ginger
    (if young, leave the skin on)
¼ teaspoon sesame oil
2 teaspoons cornstarch
Salt
14 oz (400 g) asparagus spears, or
    7 oz (200 g) broccoli spears, trimmed

Naji Boustany ORIGIN: LEBANON

LAMB FATTEH

Fatteh is a dish of toasted bread, chickpeas, and a yogurt sauce, sometimes with meat or vegetables. This recipe comes straight from my mom's kitchen, but now it plays a part in my own story. Just a few months after I moved to New York, I made a version with beef tongue for Gastronauts: An Adventurous Eaters Club, an organization that hosts dinners prepared by guest chefs, using menus built around offal and other "strange" ingredients. I made a version with eggplant for the judges of *Chopped* on the Food Network last summer. And the positive reception I receive to these traditional Lebanese recipes continues to excite and inspire me as my career evolves here in America.

One of the things I love most about this dish is that it can be modified to suit the season and tastes. This version uses lamb, but you can omit the meat, or use roast chicken or grilled eggplant in its place.

First, cook the lamb: In a large deep saucepan with lid, heat the olive oil over medium heat. Season the lamb with salt, and brown the meat for about 4 minutes on each side, then transfer to a plate (you may need to do this in batches).

Add the onion to the pan, sprinkle with ½ teaspoon salt, and sauté until softened, about 5 minutes. Stir in the garlic and cook for a minute or two more. Return the lamb to the pan. Add a pinch of salt and pepper and the Lebanese 7-spice. Add enough hot water just to cover the shanks. Bring to a boil, lower the heat to a gentle simmer, and cook until the lamb is tender and falling from the bone, 2 to 2½ hours. Transfer the meat to a plate, reserving the stock for another use. When cool enough to handle, remove the meat from the bone and pull it into bite-size pieces.

Empty the chickpeas and their liquid into a small pot. Bring to a boil, reduce the heat, and simmer for 10 minutes to soften. Rinse, drain, and set aside.

Using a mortar and pestle, mash the garlic with a pinch of salt.

In a medium bowl, combine the yogurt, tahini, mashed garlic, cayenne, Lebanese 7-spice, olive oil, ½ teaspoon of the cumin, 1 teaspoon salt, and half of the lemon juice. Whisk until thoroughly combined.

Sprinkle the meat with the remaining cumin and lemon juice. Divide the meat between serving plates, top with the sauce, and sprinkle with the chickpeas. Scatter the toasted flatbread and pine nuts on top, and sprinkle with a light drizzle of olive oil and the Aleppo pepper.

Naji Boustany is executive chef and operations director at Manousheh, a Lebanese eatery in New York City. He was a contestant on the Food Network's *Chopped* in 2017. He was born in Beirut, Lebanon, and his family is from Deir al Qamar, in the al Chouf Mountains. He first learned to cook in his mother's kitchen, growing up to manage a local farmers' market, before overseeing the kitchen of Tawlet Souk el Tayeb, a farm-to-table restaurant in Beirut. He is co-founder of FERN, a Lebanese NGO that works to transform Beirut's restaurants into waste-free establishments.

Serves 6

14 oz (400 g) can chickpeas
3–5 garlic cloves
Salt and ground black pepper
1 cup (9 oz/250 g) plain whole
  milk yogurt
3 tablespoons tahini
1 teaspoon cayenne pepper
1 teaspoon Lebanese 7-spice
1 tablespoon extra virgin olive oil,
  plus more to garnish
1 teaspoon cumin
Juice of 1 lemon
1 large Lebanese flatbread or pita,
  toasted and broken into pieces
¼ cup (1¼ oz/35 g) pine nuts
1 teaspoon Aleppo pepper,
  to garnish (optional)

LAMB SHANKS

2 tablespoons extra virgin olive oil
4–6 free-range lamb shanks
  (3–5 lb/1.4–2.25 kg total)
Salt and pepper
1 large onion, thickly sliced
2 garlic cloves, chopped
½ teaspoon Lebanese 7-spice

Thomas Kim ORIGIN: SOUTH KOREA

DONKAAS BUTTERMILK FRIED PORK
Ton Katsu

My family emigrated from Korea and both my parents worked long hours, so mealtimes often consisted of just rice and a few different kimchi. For special occasions or as a treat, my mom would make *donkaas*, the Korean version of a Japanese staple. This dish reflects the different influences in my life and how they surface: Korean, Japanese, and American ingredients used to create unique but familiar comfort food.

This is a great dish to cook with your family because you can include them in the pounding or breading of the pork. It keeps well, so you can easily make a double portion, wrap each breaded pork loin individually, and freeze it (fry it from frozen for best results). This recipe works with chicken if you want to go a more Southern/Asian route. Also, it makes for a killer sandwich!

You will need to marinate the meat overnight, or for at least 4 hours. Look for doenjang, tonkatsu sauce, and takuan in Asian grocery stores. You can use store-bought citrus ponzu too, but my version is worth the effort.

Using a rolling pin or meat tenderizer, pound the pork loin between parchment paper or plastic wrap until it is flat and even, about ¼ inch (6 mm) thick, but be careful not to break the meat apart.

Sift the flour into a large bowl. Gradually mix in the buttermilk, doenjang, and egg, then mix until smooth. Toss the pork in the mixture until evenly coated. Marinate overnight, or for at least 4 hours.

Mix the saltines and breadcrumbs in large shallow bowl. Remove the pork from the marinade (don't wipe it off!), and coat the pork with the panko-cracker mixture, gently pressing the coating into the pork to make sure that the crust adheres to the meat.

Heat 2 inches (5 cm) oil in a frying pan over medium-high heat until the surface begins to shimmer. Cook the pork for 3 minutes on each side, until golden brown, with an internal temperature of 150°F (65°C).

Place the steamed rice in a serving bowl. In a mortar and pestle, grind the sesame and perilla seeds, if using, and sprinkle this over the rice. Serve the pork and rice with the kimchi, pickled daikon, and sauces on the side for dipping.

Serves 4

1½ lb (700 g) boneless center-cut loin, sliced into four 6 oz (170 g) portions
¼ cup (1 oz/30 g) all-purpose flour
1 cup (240 ml) buttermilk
2 tablespoons doenjang (Korean soybean paste) or miso paste
1 egg
½ cup (3½ oz/100 g) crumbled saltine crackers (about 30)
½ cup (1 oz/30 g) panko breadcrumbs
Vegetable oil, for frying

TO SERVE

2 cups (14 oz/400 g) short-grain rice, cooked according to package instructions
1 tablespoon roasted sesame seeds (optional)
1 teaspoon perilla seeds (optional)
8 oz (225 g) Napa kimchi
4 oz (115 g) takuan (pickled daikon radish) or bread-and-butter pickles
¾ cup (175 ml) ponzu (recipe right)
1 cup (240 ml) tonkatsu sauce (I recommend Bulldog brand)

TAMARIND PONZU

In a small pot, combine the soy sauce, mirin, and vinegar. Heat over medium-low until barely simmering. Add the kombu and katsuobushi, turn off the heat, and set aside to steep for 15 minutes. Add all the other ingredients, cover, and refrigerate overnight. Strain, discarding the solids.

(Pictured on page 153)

Thomas Kim is chef and owner of Rabbit Hole Restaurant in Minneapolis. He is Korean-American, born and raised in Los Angeles. He grew up eating Korean food, but his culinary background is in fine-dining Japanese cuisine. After work, he frequently ate at local taquerias and burger stands, so he and his wife set out to create a restaurant that honors all of those influences and reflects the current American culinary landscape.

Makes ¾ cup (175 ml)

¼ cup (60 ml) soy sauce
1 tablespoon mirin (Japanese sweet wine) or sweet cooking wine
1 tablespoon rice wine vinegar
3 inch (8 cm) square dashi kombu (dried seaweed)
4 teaspoons katsuobushi (Japanese dried bonito flakes)
4 teaspoons seedless tamarind paste
2 tablespoons lemon juice
1 tablespoon lime juice
1 tablespoon orange juice
1 tablespoon yuzu juice or Meyer lemon juice

DESSERTS

Curtis Stone ORIGIN: AUSTRALIA

PAVLOVA WITH COCONUT CREAM AND TROPICAL FRUIT

Pavlova is an iconic Australian dessert. This version features classic Australian flavors like passion fruit and mango, as well as the tropical flavors of coconut and pineapple, inspired by Australia's Southeast Asian immigrants. It is presented in a more unique way than traditional pavlova, as a wreath rather than one large "cake," which makes it easier to cut and serve. I created it for Christmas, which occurs during the summer in Australia. Visually, it's a stunner and a great representation of my home country, since it looks like one big, gorgeous sun.

First, make the meringue: Position the rack in the center of your oven and preheat to 300°F (150°C). Line large baking sheet with parchment paper and draw a 6 inch (15 cm) circle on the paper. Turn the paper over.

In a large bowl, or the bowl of stand mixer fitted with the whisk attachment, beat the egg whites until foamy. Gradually add the sugar, beating on medium-high speed, until firm, glossy peaks form, 10 minutes. Beat in the vinegar, vanilla, and salt. Sift the cornstarch over the meringue and gently fold it in.

Using a large ice cream scoop or spoon, dollop 12 mounds of meringue onto the prepared sheet, following the outside edge of the circle. Using the back of the scoop, smooth and flatten the top.

Place in the oven, immediately reduce the temperature to 220°F (100°C), and bake for 1 hour and 5 minutes, or until the meringue is crisp on outside but still has a marshmallow-like center, and puffs very slightly. Turn the oven off, prop the oven door open with a wooden spoon, and leave the meringue in the oven for 30 minutes, then remove and set aside to cool completely.

To assemble the pavlova wreath, scoop out the firm, thick white layer of coconut cream that collects atop the coconut water in the can, and transfer it to large chilled bowl. Reserve the coconut water for another use. Using electric handheld mixer, whip the coconut cream on high speed for 2 minutes. Gently fold in the whipped heavy cream.

Gently remove the meringue from the parchment paper and place on a large round platter. Spoon the whipped coconut cream mixture over the meringue. Spoon half of the passion fruit pulp over the cream. Decoratively arrange the mango and pineapple on top, and top with the remaining passion fruit pulp. Sprinkle with the toasted coconut.

Using a serrated knife, cut the pavlova into wedges and serve.

Serves 12

6 large egg whites, room temperature
1½ cups (10 oz/280 g) sugar
1 teaspoon distilled white vinegar
½ teaspoon pure vanilla extract
¼ teaspoon kosher salt
2 tablespoons cornstarch

TOPPING

14 oz (400 g) can organic full-fat coconut cream, chilled overnight
1 cup (240 ml) heavy cream, whipped to stiff peaks
½ cup (120 ml) passion fruit pulp, from about 8 small passion fruits
1 ripe mango (about 14 oz/400 g), peeled, pitted, and thinly sliced
¼ pineapple (9 oz/250 g), peeled, cored, and thinly sliced crosswise
½ cup (1½ oz/40 g) shaved coconut, toasted

Curtis Stone is a chef, restaurateur, media personality, businessman, and *New York Times* best-selling author. He gained his twelve years' culinary training in his native Australia, and in Europe, eight years of which were under renowned chef Marco Pierre White. He currently lives in Los Angeles, California, where he debuted his first solo restaurant, Maude, in Beverly Hills, and partnered with his brother Luke to open Gwen Butcher Shop & Restaurant in Hollywood.

Samantha Seneviratne ORIGIN: SRI LANKA

TRUE LOVE CAKE

This sticky semolina cake is the first cake I ever made in my grandmother's kitchen in Sri Lanka. The fragrant, cashew-studded treat is served throughout the country at teatime or whenever guests come calling. The dense crumb and chewy edges remind me of something that would happen if a butter cake and a blondie had a baby—a pleasingly crunchy, tender, and sweet love child. In the oven, the rose water, honey, cardamom, and cinnamon start to bloom. This cake doubles as aromatherapy.

Preheat the oven to 300°F (150°C). Butter a 9 inch (23 cm) square baking pan. Line the pan with parchment paper, leaving a 2 inch (5 cm) overhang on two sides. Butter the parchment.

In a large skillet, melt the butter over medium heat. Add the semolina and cook, stirring, until it is very lightly toasted, 2 to 3 minutes. Turn the semolina mixture out onto a large plate to cool to room temperature.

In a large bowl, with an electric mixer, beat the 6 egg yolks and sugar on medium speed until pale and thick, 3 to 4 minutes. Beat in the honey, rose water, almond extract, cinnamon, cardamom, lemon zest, and salt. Beat in the cooled semolina mixture and fold in the cashews.

With clean beaters, whip the 4 egg whites on medium speed to medium-stiff but not dry peaks, about 2 minutes. Stir one-quarter of the egg whites into the semolina mixture, then fold the remaining egg whites into this batter. Pour the batter into the prepared pan and smooth the top. Bake until golden brown and a toothpick inserted into the center comes out with moist crumbs attached, 40 to 50 minutes. Let cool completely in the pan on a rack. To serve, cut along the edges of the cake to release it from the pan. Using the parchment, transfer the cake to a cutting board and cut into diamonds. Store the cake in an airtight container at room temperature for up to 3 days.

Serves 16

¾ cup (6 oz/170 g) unsalted butter, plus more for greasing
1 cup (6 oz/170 g) coarse semolina
4 large eggs, separated, plus 2 large egg yolks
1⅓ cups (9½ oz/270 g) sugar
¼ cup (60 ml) honey
1 tablespoon rose water
¾ teaspoon almond extract
2 teaspoons ground cinnamon
1½ teaspoons freshly ground cardamom
1 teaspoon finely grated lemon zest (from 1 lemon)
¾ teaspoon kosher salt
1 cup (4½ oz/130 g) finely chopped raw cashews

Samantha Seneviratne is an author and food stylist. Her first cookbook, *The New Sugar and Spice*, was nominated for a 2016 James Beard Award. She's also the author of *Gluten Free For Good* and a contributor to various food media outlets including the *New York Times* and *Martha Stewart*. She is currently focusing on a new book and a new baby in Brooklyn.

Joan Nathan ORIGIN: POLAND, GERMANY

GERMAN PLUM TART
Zwetschgenkuchen

My father came from Augsburg, Germany, and had the good sense to leave in 1929 for the United States. Some of his relatives who stayed died in Auschwitz and Theresienstadt. My grandparents were from Poland, Austro-Hungaria, and Germany. This Southern German and Alsatian plum cake has been handed down in my family for generations. The recipe is one we all love and eat in the fall, at Rosh Hashanah, when Italian plums are in season. It can be made with other plums at other times of the year; just slice them very thinly.

First, make the pastry: To use a food processor, fit it with the metal blade. Add the flour, salt, and 1 tablespoon of the sugar and pulse to combine. Cut the butter or margarine into small pieces, add them to the bowl, and process until crumbly. Add the egg yolk and process until the dough forms a ball, adding more flour if necessary.

To make the dough by hand, combine the flour, salt, and 1 tablespoon of the sugar in a mixing bowl. Use your fingers or a pastry blender to work the butter or margarine into the dry ingredients until the mixture resembles coarse breadcrumbs. Add the egg yolk and work the dough into a ball.

Remove the dough from the bowl, dust with flour, and pat into a flattened circle. Cover with plastic wrap and refrigerate for at least 30 minutes.

When you are ready to make the crust, dust your hands and the dough with flour. Place the dough in the center of a 9 inch (23 cm) loose-bottom tart pan. Using your fingers, gently pat it out to line the pan. Trim the crust and prick the bottom in several places with the tines of a fork.

Position the rack in the center of your oven and preheat to 375°F (190°C).

Sprinkle the breadcrumbs on the crust, then spoon the apricot preserve on top, and drizzle with the brandy. Place the plum quarters on the crust in concentric circles, starting from the outside and working inward, so that each overlaps the next, until the base is completely covered. Sprinkle with the cinnamon and the remaining sugar. (At this point, if you wish, you can wrap and freeze the tart to bake it later. Just remove it from the freezer one hour before baking.)

Bake the tart in until the crust is golden and the plums are juicy, about 40 minutes. Just before serving, sprinkle with confectioner's sugar.

Serves 6 to 8

1 cup (4½ oz/125 g) unbleached all-purpose flour, plus more for dusting
Pinch salt
¼ cup (1¾ oz/50 g) sugar
½ cup (4 oz/115 g) unsalted butter or pareve margarine, chilled
1 large egg yolk
2 teaspoons dried breadcrumbs
⅓ cup (3½ oz/100 g) apricot preserve
1 teaspoon brandy
2 lb (1 kg) Italian plums, quartered and pitted, or other plum varieties, thinly sliced and pitted
½ teaspoon cinnamon
Confectioner's sugar

Joan Nathan is author of eleven cookbooks, including her latest work, *King Solomon's Table: A Culinary Exploration of Jewish Cooking from around the World*, released in April 2017 by Alfred P. Knopf. Joan has received numerous awards for her cookbooks, including multiple James Beard Awards and accolades from the International Association of Culinary Professionals. She is a regular contributor to the *New York Times* and *Tablet* magazine.

Nadia Hubbi and Deana Kabakibi   ORIGIN: SYRIA

SWEET CHEESE PASTRY WITH ORANGE BLOSSOM SYRUP

Knafeh

Cooking is always an escape for me. I usually have music playing in the background as the aromas of the spices come together and transport me to another place and time. When I cook Syrian dishes, I feel the innocent days of my childhood. The coziness wraps around me.

Knafeh is one of the quintessential sweets of the region and it is always brought out for times of celebration and happiness. Sometimes baking the *knafeh* itself is the occasion that gathers my family together! The smell of the warm phyllo dough in the oven and the syrup bubbling on the stove and anxiously waiting to sink our teeth into crunchy sweetness is what it means to be a child of Syrian parents. When Deana and I discussed what dish to choose for this project and what really resonated with us, we both reminisced about our almost identical *knafeh* childhood memories.

This is a traditional recipe, but we baked the *knafeh* in cupcake form, identifying with our American upbringing. *Knafeh* is traditionally made with unsalted Arabic cheeses, which can be found in Middle Eastern supermarkets, but queso fresco is a lot easier to find and a great substitute. While this is a classic dish from Nablus, families across the Middle East make their own versions. Try it with different cheeses and combinations (ricotta, soaked feta, and mozzarella all work), or use more or less cheese depending on how cheesy you like it. You can also experiment with the shape and size of the baking tray. *Knafeh* is rarely ever made in small quantities; traditionally, it is made in a large pizza-size tray to feed many *knafeh* fans. —Nadia

Makes one 9 inch (23 cm) cake or 24 mini cakes

10 oz (280 g) queso fresco, or
  more to taste
1 lb (450 g) package shredded phyllo
  dough (kataifi), defrosted
1 cup (8 oz/225 g) unsalted butter,
  melted, plus more for greasing
½ cup (6 oz/170 g) Mexican crema or
  crème friache, or more to taste

ORANGE BLOSSOM SYRUP
1 cup (240 ml) water
2 cups (14 oz/400 g) sugar
1 teaspoon lemon juice
1-2 teaspoons orange blossom water
  (optional)

TO SERVE (OPTIONAL)
Edible dried rose petals
Ground pistachios

First, make the syrup: In a small saucepan, combine the water and sugar. Bring to a boil over medium heat, stirring with a wooden spoon to dissolve the sugar. As soon as it boils, add the lemon juice and reduce the heat to low. Simmer for 9 minutes, until thickened slightly. Add the orange blossom water and simmer for an additional 1 minute. Remove from the heat and set aside to cool completely.

Preheat the oven to 400°F (200°C) and grease a 9 inch (23 cm) cake pan or two 12-hole cupcake pans.

In a small bowl, cover the queso fresco in warm water and soak for 5 to 7 minutes to reduce the salt. Drain, crumble the cheese, and set aside.

Working in batches, pulse the shredded phyllo dough in your food processor in short bursts until coarsely crumbled, or chop the pastry by hand. Transfer to a large bowl.

Using your hands, mix the butter into the crumbled pastry until completely absorbed.

For the cake, press two-thirds of the buttered pastry (about 4 cups) into the bottom of your cake pan. Spread it out to line the base of the pan and part-way up the sides, making a large shallow indent in the middle to within 1 inch (2 cm) of the side of the pan—this indent is very important to make sure the pastry completely encases the cheese filling.

Spread the crumbled queso fresco over the indent in the pastry. Top the queso fresco with the crema.

Sprinkle the remaining buttered pastry (about 2 cups) over the top, completely covering the cheese. Bake until the pastry is just golden on top, 15 to 20 minutes, watching carefully, since it can burn easily.

For the mini bites, press about 3 tablespoons of the shredded pastry mixture in each hole of your cupcake pans, and make a wide indent in the middle of the pastry in each hole. Equally divide the queso fresco among the indents in the pastry (about 1 tablespoon in each), and top with the crema (about 1 teaspoon in each). Top with the remaining pastry (about 2 tablespoons in each), making sure the filling is well covered. Bake until just golden on top, 10 to 12 minutes, watching carefully since they can burn easily.

Remove the pan from the oven, transfer to a plate, and immediately drizzle generously with the cooled syrup. Garnish as desired and serve warm, with any remaining syrup on the side.

(Pictured on page 165)

Nadia Hubbi is a food stylist, photographer, blogger, and founder of Sweet Pillar, a Modern Middle Eastern Food company specializing in dips, cookies, and confectionary. She writes about modern and traditional dishes handed down from her Syrian family on her blog *Sweet Pillar FOOD*. She was raised in New Jersey and currently resides in Southern California with her family.

Deana Kabakibi is co–content creator of *Sweet Pillar FOOD*. She gave up a career as a lawyer to follow her passion for cooking and baking, and hasn't looked back. She is Syrian, by way of New York, and currently lives in Los Angeles.

April Bloomfield ORIGIN: ENGLAND

BANOFFEE PIE

A quintessentially English treat invented by a couple of publicans at The Hungry Monk in East Sussex, this is the dessert I'd choose to end my final meal, the sweet I'd eat in my last moments on earth. A concoction that features layers of whipped cream, ripe bananas, and caramelized milk (perhaps more familiar as dulce de leche), this pie might sound too sugary. But somehow the cream cuts through all that sweetness, and when you eat it good and cold, it becomes one of those compulsively tasty desserts that you'll find yourself finishing in about ten seconds. Caramelizing the condensed milk is easy but takes some time, and must cool completely before you can safely open the cans. To save time, you can substitute ready-made dulce de leche. Any cooks who dread rolling out tart dough will be thrilled to learn the grated method I suggest for this recipe.

Make the caramelized milk: Place the unopened cans of condensed milk in a large pot, and add enough water to cover them by at least 1 inch (2 cm). Bring the water to a boil, lower the heat, and simmer for 4 hours, checking the water level frequently to ensure that the cans remain completely submerged the entire time (this is very important; top up with more boiling water if the level gets low). Carefully remove the cans from the pot and let them cool completely. Refrigerate until needed and bring to room temperature before using.

Make the crust: Sift the flour into a mixing bowl or the bowl of your food processor, then add the sugar, butter, and salt. Pulse or crumble the mixture until it resembles fine breadcrumbs. Add the egg yolks and mix until the egg is incorporated and you have a crumbly dough. Lightly knead by hand, just until smooth. Form the dough into a ball, wrap it in plastic wrap, and refrigerate for at least 2 hours or for up to 2 days.

Preheat the oven to 350°F (180°C).

Cut the chilled dough into 2 or 3 large pieces. Using a box grater, coarsely grate the dough onto the base of a 10 inch (25 cm) loose-bottom tart pan. Using your fingers, press the dough evenly around the base and sides of the pan, so it is about ¼ inch (6 mm) thick on the base, and ½ inch (1 cm) thick around the sides. Work quickly, before the dough warms up too much. Gently prick the bottom with a fork here and there, then chill in the freezer for 15 minutes.

Line the the dough with a 13 inch (33 cm) round of parchment paper, and fill with pie weights (or dried beans or rice). Set the pan on a baking sheet. Bake the crust until the rim is light golden brown, 15 to 20 minutes. Remove the parchment paper and weights and bake until brown all over, about 15 minutes more.

Serves 12

Two unopened 14 oz (400 g) cans
  condensed milk, labels removed
8–10 bananas
2 cups (480 ml) heavy cream
3 tablespoons confectioner's sugar,
  or to taste
1 vanilla bean, split lengthwise
3 tablespoons grated bittersweet
  chocolate

CRUST
1½ cups (7 oz/200 g) all-purpose flour
½ cup (2 oz/60 g) confectioner's sugar
½ cup (4 oz/115 g) unsalted butter, cut
  into ¼ inch (6 mm) pieces and chilled
¼ teaspoon salt
2 large egg yolks, lightly beaten

Assemble the pie: Peel half of the bananas and slice diagonally into ½ inch (1 cm) pieces. Starting from the outside and working your way towards the center, arrange the banana slices in concentric circles on the base of the baked pastry, so each piece overlaps slightly. Gently dollop the caramelized condensed milk on top of the bananas, and spread it to evenly cover them. Cover the tart with plastic wrap and chill it in the refrigerator for 15 minutes, or up to 2 hours.

While the pie is chilling, make the whipped cream: In a large mixing bowl, combine the cream and confectioner's sugar. Using a knife, scrape the vanilla seeds into the bowl; discard the pod. Using a whisk or electric mixer, whip the cream to soft peaks. Cover and refrigerate until needed.

When you are ready to serve, remove the pie from the refrigerator. Peel and slice the remaining bananas, and add another layer of bananas to the pie. Give the chilled whipped cream a good stir and, using a pastry bag or a spatula, spread the whipped cream over the pie, so it completely covers the bananas. Sprinkle the grated chocolate over the top. Serve immediately, while it is still cold.

(Pictured on page 169 and 214)

April Bloomfield is executive chef and co-owner of The Spotted Pig, The Breslin Bar & Dining Room, The John Dory Oyster Bar, Tosca Cafe, Salvation Taco, White Gold Butchers, and most recently, The Hearth & Hound in Los Angeles, California. She won the 2014 James Beard Award for Best Chef, New York City, and was nominated for an Emmy for cohosting the second season of the PBS show *Mind of a Chef*. She is author of *A Girl and Her Pig* and *A Girl and Her Greens*. A native of Birmingham, England, she lives in New York City.

Monica Meehan ORIGIN: AUSTRIA, UK, CANADA

VANILLA SHORTBREAD CRESCENTS
Vanillekipferln

My mother and her family were refugees during the Second World War, forced to leave their charmed life in former Yugoslavia to repatriate with Austrian relatives in Graz and Vienna. A decade later, when small luxuries were accessible again—butter, sugar!—my grandmother began a yearly tradition, spanning over thirty years, of hosting a Boxing Day afternoon tea for our vast number of family and friends. The *vanillekipferln* were the first to disappear from her elegant china, and when the last guest left, the family would head off for a week-long ski trip in the Alps early the next morning, bellies filled with these magical vanilla half-moons. I attended several of these festive teas in Austria during my childhood and early twenties, and my mother still maintains this tradition each Christmas in Canada, where she lives today.

Preheat the oven to 350°F (180°C). Line a baking sheet with parchment paper.

Sift the flour into the bowl of a food processor and add the confectioner's sugar and vanilla sugar. Dice the butter; add it to the flour, and process until the mixture resembles coarse breadcrumbs. Add the ground almonds and the egg yolks and process again. Turn the mixture out onto a clean, floured work surface and, using your hands, mix swiftly into a smooth dough.

Wrap the dough in plastic wrap and refrigerate for one hour. After this time, remove from the fridge, remove the plastic wrap, and break off small walnut-size pieces of dough. On a clean work surface, roll them into ½ inch by 2½ inch (1 cm by 6 cm) rolls. Bend into crescents and arrange on the prepared baking sheet, spacing them about 1½ inches (4 cm) apart. Bake for 18 to 20 minutes, until golden.

In the meantime, prepare the coating: sift all three sugars into a large bowl and mix well.

When cooked, remove the crescents from the oven and immediately tip them into the coating, carefully rolling them in the sugar to coat them all over. (You may have to work in batches, depending on the size of your bowl.) This is an art indeed, since you have to work quickly while the crescents are still hot!

Once the crescents are all coated and still a little warm, arrange them in a cookie tin with a tight-fitting lid, placing a sheet of wax paper between each layer. Let them cool in the tin with the lid on. They are not suitable for freezing, but they can be stored for up to four weeks.

Makes 4 dozen

2¼ cups (10 oz/280 g) all-purpose flour, plus more for dusting
½ cup (2 oz/60 g) confectioner's sugar
1 tablespoon vanilla sugar (store bought or homemade; recipe right)
Scant 1 cup (7½ oz/215 g) unsalted butter, cold
1 cup (3½ oz/100 g) ground almonds
2 small egg yolks

FOR THE COATING
2 cups (8½ oz/240 g) confectioner's sugar
⅓ cup (1½ oz/40 g) vanilla sugar
3 tablespoons sugar

HOMEMADE VANILLA SUGAR

Fill an 8 oz (225 g) glass jar with confectioner's sugar. Run the blade of a sharp knife down the length of a vanilla bean to split it open. Cut these two lengths again. Do not scrape out the seeds! Place the lengths into the confectioner's sugar in the jar and seal. The sugar will take on the vanilla's essence within a month, producing a lovely aromatic flavor. Vanilla sugar keeps for up to 6 months in a sealed jar and can be used as a replacement for the packaged variety, which has very little flavor.

(Pictured on page 172)

Monica Meehan has spent her life exploring her diverse roots and passion for food, travel, and culture. Raised in Canada by her Austrian mother and British father, she resided in London for over a decade, before relocating to New York City, where she continues a successful career in publishing. Her internationally celebrated cookbook, *The Viennese Kitchen*, is rich with her family's affluent history and sumptuous recipes, against the breathtaking backdrop of turn-of-the-century Vienna.

Makes 1 cup (4oz/115g)

1 vanilla bean
1 cup (4 oz/115 g) confectioner's sugar

Dalia Mortada ORIGIN: SYRIA

SWEET SESAME SNAPS
Barazek

In Syria, the exchange of sweets between friends, family, and neighbors is tradition, especially during the holidays. It's not so different from exchanging cookies for Christmas or having a crowd at your dinner table for Thanksgiving. One of my favorite cookies is *barazek*, which is a crunchy, ginger snap–thin cookie pressed into pistachio and doused in sesame seeds. My family would always get boxes of sweets—including these cookies—directly from Damascus. Friends or relatives who recently came from the ancient city would deliver tightly plastic-wrapped boxes from our favorite bakeries. Each bite of these cookies reminds me of my mom plucking *barazek* out of a tin full of other tasty treats. "They're so addictive," she'd say through crunching.

Traditionally, vegetable or cow's ghee is the fat of choice for Syrian sweets. Cow's ghee is simply butter without the milk solids and water, creating a richer flavor. I highly recommend using vegetable ghee because it has a less imposing flavor. If you don't have any ghee at all, then you can use butter. I prefer these cookies to be less sweet, especially since there's a syrup coating on top, but this recipe works fine with ¼ cup (1¾ oz/50 g) more sugar, if you so desire.

First, make the syrup: In a small saucepan, combine the sugar and water and bring to a boil. Reduce the heat to low, and simmer until the sugar dissolves, about 3 minutes. Set aside and let cool.

In a medium-size bowl or the bowl of your stand mixer, cream the butter and sugar together. Mix in the mahlab (if using) and baking powder. Add the flour and yeast, and mix until you have a uniform mealy texture. Mixing continuously, gradually add the milk.

Use your hands to gather the dough into a ball at the bottom of the bowl. Cover it loosely with a towel or plastic wrap and let it rest for about 15 minutes, or up to an hour.

Meanwhile, toast the sesame seeds in a dry pan over medium heat until lightly golden. Keep a close eye, because they burn easily!

Position the racks in the center of your oven and preheat to 325°F (160°C). Line 2 to 4 baking sheets with parchment paper.

On a small flat plate, pour just enough syrup to cover the surface. Sprinkle with just enough sesame seeds to cover the surface of the syrup. Set aside the remaining syrup and sesame seeds; you'll need them throughout the process. On another small, flat plate, spread a thin layer of pistachios. You want only a few pieces of pistachios to make it onto your cookies. Set aside the remaining pistachios; you'll need to replenish them as you go.

Once the dough has rested, roll it into teaspoon-sized balls. Using the palm of your hand, flatten one dough ball into a round until pretty thin, but thick enough to be handled easily (about ¼ inch/6 mm).

Makes 4½ dozen

¾ cup (6 oz/170 g) ghee or butter
½ cup (3½ oz/100 g) sugar
½ teaspoon ground mahlab (ground
    St. Lucy's cherry seeds; optional)
1 teaspoon baking powder
2½ cups (11 oz/315 g) all-purpose flour
1 teaspoon instant yeast
⅓ cup (75 ml) low-fat milk, at room
    temperature
¾ cup (4 oz/115 g) sesame seeds,
    toasted
½ cup (2 oz/60 g) raw pistachios,
    sliced

SYRUP
¼ cup (1¾ oz/50 g) sugar
¼ cup (60 ml) water

Press the round into the pistachios. Then flip it over, and press it into the plate of syrup and sesame seeds. You want a really nice coating of sesame seeds. If you have blank spots, sprinkle some on top. Transfer to your baking sheet sesame-side up, leaving 1 inch (2 cm) around each cookie. Repeat the process, adding more syrup, seeds, and nuts to your plates as they get used up.

Bake for 25 to 30 minutes, or until the edges are golden and crisp, rotating halfway through. Keep a close eye after around the 18 minute mark, since oven temperatures vary, and these cookies can burn easily. You may need to bake in batches. The cookies will keep in an airtight container for about two weeks, but they probably won't last that long!

(Pictured on page 173)

Dalia Mortada is an American journalist of Syrian heritage. She has spent recent years telling stories of Syrians now in the Diaspora through the lens of food, for her special project *Savoring Syria*. She also hosts dining events for Syrians and their new communities in cities throughout the US and Europe, as a way to break down barriers by breaking bread. She lives in Virginia.

Paulina Farro ORIGIN: PHILIPPINES

SWEET COCONUT SOUP
Ginataang Bilo Bilo

Ginataang is a Filipino sweet coconut soup, served warm, and usually filled with jackfruit, yams, and glutinous rice balls. This recipe brings me back to many a backyard baby shower or birthday party, *lechon* and *lumpia* likely stacked sky high in the corner, but I'd head straight for the *ginataang* because those chewy glutinous rice balls were so much fun to eat.

Look for saba bananas, jackfruit, and glutinous rice flour (also labeled sweet rice flour or mochiko) in specialty food stores and Asian grocery stores. Traditionally, the dish uses Filipino ube yams, but sweet potatoes work just as well. If you can't find saba bananas, use regular banana, and you can use mango in place of the jackfruit, if desired.

Make your glutinous rice balls: In a large mixing bowl, combine the glutinous rice flour with ¼ cup (60 ml) water and mix to a firm dough, first with a spoon, and then with your hands. If the mixture is too crumbly, slowly mix in more water 1 tablespoon at a time until it becomes more pliable. If it is too sticky, you can add more rice flour 1 tablespoon at a time. You can color a portion of the dough with food coloring, if desired.

Break off a 1 inch (2 cm) piece of dough, and roll it between the palms of your hands to make a small uniform ball. Repeat with the rest of the dough. Cover the balls with plastic wrap and set aside.

In a large pot, combine the sugar, jackfruit, coconut milk, and 3 cups (700 ml) water and bring to a boil. Lower heat the heat to medium-low, cover the pot, and simmer until the jackfruit is tender, about 10 minutes.

Add the glutinous rice balls, yam, and bananas, and cook for 5 minutes. Mix in the coconut cream and continue to simmer until the rice balls rise to the top, and the yam is tender, 5 to 10 minutes. Serve warm.

Serves 12

1 cup (6 oz/170 g) glutinous rice flour
Purple food coloring (optional)
2 cups (14 oz/400 g) sugar
1 cup (5½ oz/150 g) sliced jackfruit or mango
Three 14 oz (400 ml) cans coconut milk
1 cup (5 oz/140 g) finely diced purple or orange yam or sweet potato
2 saba bananas or 1 regular banana, sliced
½ cup (120 ml) coconut cream

Paulina Farro is a food writer, blogger, and illustrator eating her way around the world. She infuses her recipes with the foods she discovers on her travels, writing about them for her blog *Potato Chips are Not Dinner*, which is a finalist in the 2017 *Saveur* blog awards. As a second-generation immigrant, it is her passion to bring Filipino food to the forefront of the culinary world. When her mother came to the United States from the Philippines, she was told to only speak English and do whatever she could to fit into American culture, erasing many of her recipes and traditions. Paulina strives to bring those back through her writing, illustrations, and recipes.

Nadia Hassani ORIGIN: TUNISIA, GERMANY

IMMIGRANT CHALLAH

This yeasted fruit-filled sweet bread has something of everything that makes up my heritage and my life in America: the dough of the traditional Jewish Sabbath bread, a family favorite from my husband's side; rhubarb, which is popular in Germany, a favorite of mine since childhood, and now grows in my garden; and a distinct orange flavor, which for me is indelibly linked with the oranges in my Tunisian grandmother's courtyard. Rhubarb-orange jam is also a specialty in Pennsylvania Dutch country, where I live. This challah makes our life come full circle.

I have also made this challah with orange-flavored German plum butter (*Pflaumenmus*) or with blueberry jam, both of which are equally delicious. The mock braid technique is not only decorative, but it also prevents the jam from oozing out. This recipe makes extra rhubarb jam, so you will have leftovers.

First, make the rhubarb jam filling: Place the rhubarb in a heavy non-reactive saucepan with 2 to 3 tablespoons water. Place over medium-low heat, cover the pot, and cook until the rhubarb is soft and falling apart, about 10 minutes. Stir often at the beginning to prevent it from sticking to the bottom of the pan.

Add the orange juice, zest, and sugar and cook uncovered for 1 hour, or until the rhubarb jam is no longer runny, and the cooking spoon leaves a trail. Remove from the heat and add the orange extract. Cool and use right away, or pour the hot jam into a sterilized jar, cool, then refrigerate until ready to use.

Next, make the challah: Combine the yeast with the lukewarm water in a small bowl and let it stand for 10 minutes, until frothy.

In a large bowl, or the bowl of an electric mixer fitted with the kneading attachment, combine the flour, salt, and sugar. Add the beaten egg, yeast mixture, and oil, and knead at a slow speed to a smooth dough that comes away from the bowl, about 2 minutes. Cover and let stand for 2 hours in a warm place, until it has doubled in size.

On a floured surface, knead the dough briefly to remove any air pockets. Place a large piece of parchment paper on your work surface and lightly dust it with flour. Roll the dough into a 10 inch by 15 inch (25 cm by 40 cm) rectangle. Using the tip of a sharp knife, lightly mark two lines along the length of the dough, to divide the rectangle into three sections of equal width.

Spread a generous cup (9 oz/250 g) of the filling onto the middle section of the dough, leaving 1 to 1¼ inches (2 to 3 cm) of exposed dough on both short ends (refrigerate any leftover jam and use within 2 to 3 weeks). Using a pastry wheel, make diagonal cuts that angle towards you, at ¾ inch (18 mm) intervals, along the right side section of the dough, and leaving ½ inch (1 cm) between the cuts and the filling. Repeat this on the left side section of the dough, so you have a fishbone arrangement.

Makes 1 loaf

RHUBARB JAM FILLING
1¼ pounds (570 g) pink rhubarb,
   cut into chunks
¼ cup (60 ml) orange juice
Zest of 1 organic orange
1¼ cups (9 oz/250 g) sugar
2 teaspoons orange extract

DOUGH
1½ teaspoons active-dry yeast
½ cup plus 1½ teaspoons (125 ml)
   lukewarm water
2⅔ cups (11½ oz/330 g) all-purpose
   flour
¼ teaspoon salt
2 tablespoons sugar
1 egg, beaten, plus 1 egg, for glazing
2 tablespoons vegetable oil
Swedish pearl sugar, for sprinkling
   (optional)

Starting at one end, gently lift a cut strip of dough and place it all the way over the filling. Continue, alternating strips from the right section and the left section of the dough. When all of the strips have been used, pinch both ends of the braid together to seal, and tuck them under. Carefully transfer the parchment paper, with the braid, onto a baking sheet. Cover and let stand for 45 minutes in a warm place.

Preheat the oven to 350°F (180°C). Lightly beat the remaining egg with 2 teaspoons water. Just before baking, brush the braid with the egg wash and sprinkle it with the pearl sugar, if using. Bake in the preheated oven for 30 to 40 minutes, or until golden brown. Let cool completely on a wire rack before cutting.

(Pictured on page 180 and 213)

Nadia Hassani is the author of the book and blog, *Spoonfuls of Germany: German Regional Cuisine*, and the blog, *Green Card Gardener*. She is a copywriter, editor, and translator. She was born in Germany to a German mother and a Tunisian father, and immigrated to the United States as an adult in the late 1990s. In her garden in rural Pennsylvania, she grows many fruits and vegetables for the dishes of her mixed heritage.

Dominique Ansel ORIGIN: FRANCE

MINI MADELEINES

One of my earliest food memories from my childhood in France is visiting the local bakery with my mom and grandmother, sometimes up to three times a day, to pick up fresh bread that had just come out of the oven. There's nothing like biting into something that's just baked and still warm. In our bakeries, we pipe and bake our mini madeleines to order for our guests, so you can enjoy them when they're still hot from the oven. So many of us have memories of baking in the kitchen with our families, whether it's a cookie that's still gooey and warm, or eating a slice of pie at Thanksgiving right as it hits the dinner table. For me, baking is about emotions and creating memories. These madeleines take under 5 minutes to bake, and eating them fresh makes all the difference. You will need a nonstick mini madeleine pan for this recipe, and the batter must rest overnight.

Makes 100

½ cup (4 oz/115 g) unsalted butter
1 tablespoon dark brown sugar
2 teaspoons honey
½ cup (3½ oz/100 g) granulated sugar
½ teaspoon kosher salt, or use table salt
1 cup (4½ oz/125 g) all-purpose flour, sifted
½ teaspoon baking powder
3 large eggs, at room temperature
Grated zest of ½ lemon
Grated zest of ½ orange
Nonstick cooking spray
Confectioner's sugar, to serve

Make the batter: In a medium pot over low heat, melt the butter, brown sugar, and honey. Stir gently with a heatproof spatula to ensure that nothing burns. Keep the mixture warm over very low heat, or reheat later if necessary.

In a large bowl, combine the granulated sugar, salt, flour, and baking powder and mix well with a whisk. Form a well in the center of the dry ingredients and add the eggs one by one, whisking to incorporate each before adding the next. (The eggs must be room temperature to avoid cooling the batter; if too cold, the butter may congeal.)

When the eggs are fully incorporated and the batter is smooth, slowly whisk in the warm butter mixture. Whisk in the lemon and orange zests. The batter will still be runny, and similar in consistency to cake batter. Cover with plastic wrap, pressed directly onto the surface of the batter, to prevent a skin from forming. Refrigerate overnight to rest. You can keep the batter, covered in plastic wrap in a sealed airtight container, for up to 3 days.

The day you would like to serve, place the rack in the center of the oven and preheat to 375°F (190°C). (If your oven has a convection setting, use it, and adjust the temperature to 350°F/180°C.)

Using a rubber spatula, place 2 large scoops of batter in a piping bag so that it is one-third full. Push the batter down toward the tip of the bag. Cut an opening about ½ inch (1 cm) straight across the tip of the bag.

Hold the cooking spray about 4 inches (10 cm) away from a nonstick mini madeleine pan and spray evenly in all the cavities.

Holding the piping bag upright, about ½ inch (1 cm) above the pan, pipe the madeleine batter into the cavities so that it fills each one about three-quarters of the way.

Bake the madeleines for 2 to 2½ minutes on the center rack. When you see the batter puff up in the center, rotate the pan 180 degrees. Bake for 2 to 2½ minutes more, until the sides of the madeleines are golden blond and the center has set. Unmold immediately: bang the corner or sides of the madeleine pan against your work surface so that the fresh madeleines drop out. Sift confectioner's sugar evenly over the fresh-baked madeleines and eat immediately (do not wait more than even a few minutes!).

Repeat with the rest of the batter. If you find that the madeleines stick to the pan, try using a bit more cooking spray for the next batch, and be sure to wash the pan thoroughly between batches.

(Pictured on page 181)

Dominique Ansel is a James Beard Award–winning pastry chef and owner of eponymous bakeries in New York, Tokyo, and London, with a forthcoming restaurant opening in Los Angeles in the fall of 2017. He has created some of the most fêted pastries in the world, including the Cronut®, named one of *TIME* magazine's "25 Best Inventions of 2013." For his prolific creativity, he was named the World's Best Pastry Chef in 2017 by the World's 50 Best Restaurants awards. *Food & Wine* has called him a "Culinary Van Gogh" while the *New York Post* coined him "the Willy Wonka of New York." He was also named *Business Insider*'s "Most Innovative People Under 40," one of *Crain's* "40 under 40," and was bestowed the prestigious l'Ordre du Mérite Agricole, France's second-highest honor. Prior to opening his own shop, Dominique served as the executive pastry chef for restaurant DANIEL, when the team earned its coveted third Michelin star and a four-star review from the *New York Times*.

Ana Sofía Peláez ORIGIN: CUBA

CORNMEAL PUDDING

Harina Dulce

My family couldn't take much with them when they emigrated from Cuba. Sentiment gave way to pragmatism, so the few personal objects they managed to bring—half-finished photo albums, a worn rosary, old letters—became the relics I used to understand the world they'd left behind. It was a story that repeated itself when I was researching my book on Cuban food, and I relied on friends to share their own family's cookbooks and recipes. That was how a copy of *Delicias de La Mesa* by Maria Antonieta Reyes Gavilan y Moenck found its way to me. Published in 1925, the tattered cover barely holds the frayed pages together, and a small part of it disappears with each reading, but it inspired this recipe for *harina dulce*: slow-cooked cornmeal simmered with spices and dotted with dried fruit. Comforting and soothing, it's no less sentimental for being infinitely practical.

In a heavy pot, combine the cornmeal, evaporated milk, water, sugar, cinnamon sticks, and star anise, and whisk until well combined. Cook over low heat, stirring constantly so no lumps form, until the cornmeal thickens but is still creamy and smooth, 20 to 30 minutes. Remove from the heat and stir in the vanilla.

Divide the cooked cornmeal into individual bowls or ramekins while still warm. Top with the dried fruit and almonds (or these can be mixed in), and sprinkle with cinnamon and confectioner's sugar, to taste. Serve warm or at room temperature.

Ana Sofía Peláez is a Miami-based food writer covering the spectrum of Latin American cuisine on her blog, *Hungry Sofia*. The site has been featured by *InStyle* and *Food 52*, and was nominated by *Saveur* as one of the best regional cuisine blogs of 2012. Her work has appeared in *Smithsonian Journeys* magazine and NBCNews.com, among other national outlets. Her first cookbook, *The Cuban Table* (St. Martin's Press) was nominated for a James Beard Award in 2015.

Serves 4 to 6

1 cup (4½ oz/130 g) fine yellow
    cornmeal
2 cups (480 ml) evaporated milk
2 cups (480 ml) water
⅓ cup (2½ oz/70 g) sugar
2 cinnamon sticks
1 star anise
½ teaspoon vanilla extract

TO SERVE

1 cup (5½ oz/150 g) dried fruit, such
    as raisins, prunes, cherries, and/or
    chopped figs
Toasted almonds
Ground cinnamon
Confectioner's sugar

SNACKS AND SIDE DISHES

Tunde Wey   ORIGIN: NIGERIA

JOLLOF RICE

Jollof rice is Nigeria's national dish—well that may be a slight exaggeration, but it's pretty popular. There's a friendly rivalry between a few West African countries as to who makes the best jollof rice. The provenance of the dish is disputed, but there is evidence to suggest it originated from the Sengalese *thieboudienne*, though most Nigerians would disagree. Suffice it to say, we take jollof rice very seriously.

Jollof rice reflects a variety of important West African cooking techniques, such as stewing, steaming, smoking, and one-pot cooking. It is mostly eaten with sweet fried plantains, and chicken, goat, or beef. Some people say that the plantains have to be plentiful, and cut and fried in 1 inch (2 cm) cubes, to create the perfect balance of sweet and savory.

It is a fun dish to make, but requires some practice to get exactly right. The perfect plate of jollof rice must be slightly smoky, deeply flavored, al dente, and bright red. It's a challenge, but definitely worth it!

My cooking is always an opportunity to express the deep culinary heritage of my people, and the cross-ethnic influences that have created my unique perspective. I am happy to share this with you.

In a blender or food processor, combine the onion, tomatoes, and chili pepper, and purée. Pour half of the purée into a bowl and set aside. Add the bell peppers to the machine and pulse until smooth. Add the purée to the blended vegetables in the bowl, and stir to combine.

Place the rice in a sieve and rinse under running water until the water runs more-or-less clear.

In a medium pot, heat the vegetable oil over medium heat. Add the blended vegetables, along with the salt and jollof spices. Bring the mixture to a boil.

Add the rice and stir until well mixed, then reduce the heat to low. Tightly cover the pot and cook until the rice is al dente, about 45 minutes. Check after 25 to 30 minutes; if the rice is sauce-logged, remove the lid to cook off the excess liquid. If the rice seems dry, stir in up to 1 to 2 cups (240 to 480 ml) water. Allow the rice at the bottom of the pot to char a bit to infuse the dish with a smoky flavor. Remove from the heat and fluff with a fork.

Tunde Wey is a Nigerian cook and writer. He moved to the United States at 16. Since 2016, he has been traveling across the country with his pop-up dinner series, Blackness in America, which explores race in America from the Black perspective, through food and discussion. You can read more about his projects at FromLagos.com. He currently resides in New Orleans.

Serves 6 to 8

½ medium red onion, coarsely chopped
10 oz (280 g) tomatoes (2 medium-large), coarsely chopped
½ medium Scotch bonnet or Habanero chili pepper, stem removed
15 oz (425 g) red bell peppers (3 medium-large), coarsely chopped
2½ cups (1 lb/480 g) medium-grain rice
½ cup (120 ml) vegetable oil
1½ teaspoons salt
Fresh thyme, to garnish (optional)

JOLLOF SPICES

½ teaspoon turmeric
½ teaspoon ground coriander
½ teaspoon cumin
½ teaspoon allspice
1½ teaspoons ground hot chili pepper, such as African dried chili or cayenne
1½ teaspoons garlic powder
1½ tablespoons onion powder
2 bay leaves
½ teaspoon ground ginger
1 tablespoon dried thyme

Einat Admony ORIGIN: ISRAEL

FENUGREEK FRIED BREAD

My father used to bring this fried bread home after synagogue, and almost immediately the entire apartment would fill with the earthy aroma. Fenugreek leaves give this bread a robust flavor that rivals the vibrant yellow color. There's no need to add a spread, but if you'd like, try dipping it in yogurt.

If you can't find fenugreek leaves at a Middle Eastern grocery store, you can grind a mixture of 1 tablespoon fenugreek seeds and 2 tablespoons dried mint.

In a large bowl, whisk together the flour, fenugreek leaves, salt, turmeric, and 2 tablespoons of the sugar. Make a large well in the center of the bowl and add the yeast, the remaining 1 tablespoon sugar, and ¼ cup (60 ml) of the warm water. Let the mixture stand until foamy, about 10 minutes.

In a small bowl, combine the remaining ½ cup (120 ml) warm water and 1 tablespoon canola oil and pour this into the fenugreek mixture, mixing to combine.

Sprinkle some flour on your work surface, scrape the dough out of the bowl, and knead it until smooth and elastic. Slick a separate bowl with a little bit of oil and place the dough inside. Cover with a damp cloth and let it rise in a warm place until doubled in size, about 40 minutes.

Meanwhile, in a deep skillet or pot, heat 2 inches (5 cm) canola oil for frying over medium-high heat, until a small piece of bread sizzles upon contact with the oil.

Dust your hands and the work surface with flour. To shape the bread, cut a golf ball-size piece (about 2 inches/5 cm) from the dough and form it into a disk about the size of your palm. Repeat with the rest of the dough and line up the disks on the floured surface. When the oil is hot enough, gently drop the disks into the pan one by one. Always work in small batches to keep your oil from cooling too much. Fry the bread for 1 to 2 minutes, turn them over, and cook for another 1 minute, until golden brown. Using tongs, transfer the cooked bread to a plate lined with paper towels until cool enough to eat.

Makes about 16

2 cups (9 oz/250 g) all-purpose flour, plus more for dusting
2 tablespoons dried fenugreek leaves
1 tablespoon kosher salt
1 teaspoon ground turmeric
3 tablespoons sugar
1 tablespoon (½ oz/14 g) active-dry yeast
¾ cup (180 ml) warm water
Canola oil

Einat Admony is chef and owner of Balaboosta, Bar Bolonat, Taïm, and Kish-Kash in New York City, and author of *Balaboosta: Bold Mediterranean Recipes to Feed the People You Love*. Einat was born in Israel to a Yemenite father and a Persian mother.

Ron Duprat ORIGIN: HAITI

ISLAND SLAW

The cuisine of Haiti originates from a blend of several cooking styles, strongly influenced by Afro-Cuban and French culinary traditions. Growing up in Haiti, we ate hot slaw daily, and it always brings childhood memories. This recipe is a mix of Haitian culinary heritage, American ingredients, and my grandmother's special touch. It is great served alongside grilled fish and meats, especially pork.

Make the dressing: In a medium bowl, combine the yogurt, lime juice, cider vinegar, sugar, cilantro, cumin, salt, pepper, and chili, if using, and whisk to combine. Refrigerate for at least 30 minutes to allow the flavors to develop.

When ready to serve, combine the white cabbage, scallions, red pepper, and sliced onion in a large bowl, and add the dressing. Toss gently but thoroughly to combine. Season with additional salt and pepper, if necessary.

Ron Duprat is best known from Bravo TV's *Top Chef*, *Iron Chef America*, and *Bar Rescue*. His cuisine combines the rich flavors of his Caribbean heritage with French accents. Duprat has been featured on *The View*, *BET*, *Gourmet*, *Elle*, *Bon Appetit*, *Essence*, the *Root*, *O the Oprah Magazine*, and was one of *Ebony*'s "Top Chefs, 2015." The *Huffington Post* recognized him as one of "10 Black Chefs that are Changing the Food World." Ron is a member of the U.S. State Department's Chef Corps for Diplomatic Culinary Partnership, and has prepared meals for President and First Lady Obama, Jay Z and Beyoncé, Usher, and many more. He's affiliated with several major causes, including fighting childhood obesity, Michelle Obama's "Let's Move" campaign, No Hungry Kids, The Black Culinarian Alliance (BCA), The Word and Actions, World Central Kitchen, and Clean Cook Stove.

Serves 4

3 cups (7 oz/200 g) shredded white
    cabbage
4 scallions, thinly sliced diagonally
1 red bell pepper, thinly sliced
1 red onion, thinly sliced
Salt and ground black pepper

DRESSING

1 cup (9 oz/250 g) plain yogurt
3 tablespoons lime juice
2 tablespoons cider vinegar
2 tablespoons sugar
1 tablespoon chopped cilantro leaves
1 teaspoon ground cumin
1 teaspoon salt
½ teaspoon ground black pepper
1–2 Habanero or other chili peppers,
    cored, seeded, and finely chopped
    (optional)

Nina Compton ORIGIN: SAINT LUCIA

ROASTED JERK CORN

This is a signature dish at my restaurant and a nod to my heritage. It is a combination of my Caribbean roots and my training in Italian cuisine. Jerk seasoning is a staple in St. Lucia and this dish is inspired by my childhood spent there.

First, make the jerk butter: In a medium bowl, combine all of the spices. Fold in the butter and garlic, mixing until fully combined.

Next, make the mayonnaise: Place the egg yolk in the bowl of your food processor. Add the mustard and lemon juice, and pulse until well combined. With the motor running, add the oil very gradually in a slow, steady stream. The mixture should emulsify. Season with salt and pepper to taste.

Preheat the oven to 375°F (190°C), or prepare your grill.

Shuck and trim the corn and cut each ear into halves or pieces. Boil a large kettle of water. Place the corn in a large pot and fill with enough boiling water to cover. Boil for 2 to 3 minutes, drain, and set aside.

When cool enough to handle, generously brush each piece with jerk butter to coat, and wrap it in foil. Place on a baking sheet to roast in the oven, or place on your grill. Cook for 6 to 8 minutes, or until tender.

Meanwhile, combine the ranch breadcrumb ingredients and set aside.

Once cooked, remove the corn pieces from the foil, and brush with jerk butter again. Place on a serving plate and top each piece with a dollop of the mayonnaise. Sprinkle with the ranch breadcrumbs and chopped chives.

Dip the lime wedges in cayenne pepper, if desired, and serve alongside the corn. You can store any leftover mayonnaise or jerk butter for about a week.

A native of St. Lucia, **Nina Compton** is chef and owner of Compère Lapin in New Orleans, which received a rave review in the *New York Times*, and was listed in the top 10 of *Playboy*'s "Best New Bars in America, 2016," and named Best New Restaurant by *New Orleans Magazine* and *Times-Picayune*. In 2017, she was a finalist for a James Beard Award for Best Chef, South, and *Food & Wine* named her as one of their "Best New Chefs in America." In addition to the success of her first restaurant, Nina is also currently the culinary ambassador of St. Lucia.

Serves 6 to 8

6–8 ears of corn
1 teaspoon chopped chives or
    finely sliced scallions
2 limes, cut into wedges
Cayenne pepper (optional)

JERK BUTTER

1–1½ teaspoons cayenne pepper
1 teaspoon onion powder
1 teaspoon dried thyme
1 teaspoon sugar
1 teaspoon cumin
1 teaspoon salt
½ teaspoon paprika
½ teaspoon ground allspice
¼ teaspoon ground black pepper
¼ teaspoon dried crushed red pepper
¼ teaspoon ground nutmeg
Pinch ground cinnamon
½ cup (4 oz/115 g) butter, softened
1 large garlic clove, roasted and minced,
    or just minced

MAYONNAISE

1 large egg yolk
½ teaspoon Dijon mustard
2 teaspoons lemon juice
½ cup (120 ml) vegetable oil
Salt and ground black pepper

RANCH BREADCRUMBS

½ cup (1 oz/30 g) toasted panko
    breadcrumbs
2 tablespoons ranch dry seasoning mix
½ teaspoon crumbled crispy chicken
    skin (optional)

Katrina Jazayeri   ORIGIN: IRAN

IRANIAN SPICED PICKLES
Torshi

Torsh is the Farsi word for sour; and *torshi* is a pickle made from vegetables, herbs, and spices. It is served with rich stews and soups in the Persian tradition. When my mom traveled to Iran in 1979 to marry my dad, she would steal away to the cellar where the *torshi* was stored, and essentially ate nothing else (she doesn't really like rice, the main staple of Persian cuisine). When my Iranian aunts visit us, they fill the kitchen counters with chopped vegetables and herbs laid out on pillowcases, as they prepare a year's worth of *torshi* to leave behind for us. Look for dried limes in Middle Eastern grocery stores. You can use four pint-size (425 g) jars, two quart-size (1 kg) jars, or any nonreactive containers with tight-fitting lids. You can easily halve or double this recipe.

Preheat the oven to 350°F (180°C) and line a baking sheet with parchment paper. Salt the eggplant pieces and place them on the prepared pan. Bake for 15 minutes, then remove from the oven and allow to cool.

In a large mixing bowl, combine the eggplant pieces with the rest of the vegetables and herbs and mix well.

In a large nonreactive pot, bring the vinegar to a boil, then pour the vinegar over the vegetables in the bowl, mixing to coat them well. Let the mixture cool to room temperature.

Pack the cooled mixture into jars or containers, making sure there is a chili in each one, and store in the refrigerator. The pickles are ready to eat after one day. They'll keep for 2 to 3 weeks in the refrigerator.

(Also pictured on page 198)

Katrina Jazayeri is co-owner, with partner chef Joshua Lewin, of Juliet, named one of *Bon Appetit*'s "50 Best New Restaurants in America." Born in Queens, New York, to an Iranian father and an American mother who were brought together by food, she saw firsthand its power to create relationships, memories, and lasting connections. At 26 years old, Katrina was awarded one of 19 *Eater* Young Guns Awards in 2016, and was named one of *Zagat*'s "30 under 30" in 2014. Juliet is Boston's first tip-free restaurant. Katrina and Josh apply their commitment to social justice to their business to create a supportive work environment, featuring a profit-sharing model in favor of the traditional restaurant wage structure.

Makes 2 quarts (2 liters)

1 eggplant, peeled and diced
Salt
1 dried lime, crushed
1 teaspoon nigella seeds
1 teaspoon fennel seeds
1 teaspoon coriander seeds
3 garlic cloves, halved
2 tablespoons kosher salt
1 whole Thai bird's eye chili pepper
   per jar or container
½ teaspoon turmeric
1 large carrot, peeled and finely diced
1 large cucumber, peeled and
   finely diced
1 green bell pepper, finely diced
½ cauliflower, washed, cut into florets
2 celery stalks, sliced
½ cup (1¼ oz/35 g) shredded white
   cabbage
¼ cup (½ oz/15 g) finely chopped
   parsley
¼ cup (½ oz/15 g) finely chopped
   cilantro
¼ cup (½ oz/15 g) finely chopped dill
2½ cups (600 ml) distilled white vinegar

Lauryn Chun ORIGIN: SOUTH KOREA

STUFFED CABBAGE KIMCHI
Poggi Kimchi

This is the most traditional version of cabbage kimchi made during *kimjang* (the fall cabbage harvest). *Poggi* kimchi is stuffed cabbage halves, brined overnight and then slathered with a well-seasoned stuffing paste. The beauty of *poggi* kimchi is that the cabbage half is kept intact, and only cut just prior to serving. In doing so, you release the optimal flavor and aroma and honor your guests by giving them the freshest pieces of cabbage, brimming with tangy fermentation. In a Korean household, you would never serve leftover, precut *poggi* kimchi to your guests. Instead, it would go into a soup or a stew.

Making kimchi is a very traditional process and ingredients are typically measured by hand, so don't worry too much about getting the measurements exact. If you plan to make a smaller batch, use at least one head of cabbage. The more you make, the better the fermentation will be. You will need a wide-mouth 1 gallon (4 liter) glass pickle jar or tub large enough to fit your cabbage halves. You will need to brine overnight, and ferment for 4 to 5 days.

Generously sprinkle ¼ cup (2 oz/60 g) of the salt over the cabbage halves, making sure there is salt on the core, the outer base, the thickest parts, and between the individual leaves. Stack the cabbage halves in a large bowl or a wide, deep stockpot, layering the halves on top of one another. Set aside for 30 minutes to dry brine. Fill the bowl or pot with just enough cold water to cover the cabbage, add the remaining salt, and stir to dissolve. Taste the water—it should taste like the sea. Place a heavy plate on top of the cabbage to ensure it stays submerged, and brine at room temperature for 8 to 10 hours or overnight, turning the cabbage over midway through for even brining. As it brines, the cabbage will wilt, shrink, and sink. If, after the 10 hour brine, the outside bottom leaves are still firm, let the cabbage brine for an additional hour and check again. Brine until the leaves look bright green but wilted.

Once brined, lift the cabbage out of the water and drain. Fill another large bowl with water and rinse out the salted cabbage, gently agitating while submerged. Shake it out well and drain in a colander in the sink or over a dish rack, with the cut side facing down, for at least 40 minutes. The leaves should taste slightly salty-sweet, and the colors should look brighter than they did before brining.

Meanwhile, prepare the seasoning paste. In a small food processor fitted with a metal blade, pulse together the shrimp, anchovy sauce, garlic, ginger, and sugar until smooth. Transfer the mixture to a large bowl and mix in the chili pepper flakes and radish. Let sit for 15 minutes.

Makes 4 cabbage halves, about 16 servings

2 large heads Napa cabbage
  (6-7 lb/2.7-3 kg total), yellow leaves
  discarded, halved lengthwise
1 cup (8 oz/225 g) kosher salt, divided

SEASONING PASTE

¼ cup (2 oz/60 g) salted shrimp
¼ cup (60 ml) Korean anchovy sauce
3 tablespoons minced garlic
  (about 9 cloves)
1 tablespoon peeled, finely grated
  fresh ginger
2 teaspoons sugar
1 cup (4 oz/115 g) Korean chili pepper
  flakes (gochugaru)
1½ lb (700 g) daikon radish, (about
  1 medium), thinly sliced into
  3 inch (8 cm) strips
½ cup (120 ml) water

Take one of the cabbage halves and spread a generous amount of the seasoning paste between the leaves, working from the outermost leaf inward, and making sure the paste is applied between each layer of leaves and the innermost core. Slather the paste on the cut side of the cabbage then fold the leaves over the cut side. Repeat this process for each half.

Carefully pack the cabbage halves as tightly as possible into the jar, making sure to keep the stuffing intact. Add the water to the mixing bowl and swirl it around to collect the remaining seasoning paste; and pour it into the container. If there is a gap between the cabbage and the lid, add additional water to make sure the cabbage is fully submerged. Cover tightly. Let sit at room temperature, away from direct light, for 4 to 5 days. Refrigerate and consume within 1 year.

(Pictured on page 199)

Lauryn Chun is the author of *The Kimchi Cookbook: 60 Traditional and Modern Ways to Make and Eat Kimchi* (2012) and the founder of Mother-in-Law's Kimchi, the first line of artisanal kimchi and gochujang sauces sold in natural and specialty retailers nationally. She was inspired by the beauty of Korea's handcrafted tradition of kimchi as a fine food that belongs in the ranks of fine wine, cheese, and beer traditions. Mother-in-Law's Kimchi is based on an original recipe from her mother's 29-year-old restaurant, Jang Mo Jip (Mother-in-Law's House) in California. Mother-in-Law's Kimchi has received unprecedented press accolades in the *New York Times*, *Wall Street Journal*, *Ad Week*, *O the Oprah Magazine*, *WNYC*, *USA Today*, *Rachael Ray Every Day*, *Men's Health*, *Tasting Table*, and more, and has been featured on MSNBC and the Cooking Channel's *FoodCrafters*. Lauryn lives in Brooklyn, New York.

CONTRIBUTORS

Brenda Abdelall is an Egyptian-American, born and raised in the culturally diverse city of Ann Arbor, Michigan. Her love for Egyptian food grew each summer during her childhood visits to Egypt, which included visits to Alexandrian coastal cities, rural villages, and the growing metropolis of Al Mansoura. After watching her grandmother bake fresh bread, and her aunts roll grape leaves with perfection, Brenda has found the kitchen to be her creative outlet. She runs an award-winning Middle Eastern food blog, midEATS, and teaches Middle Eastern cooking classes in Northern Virginia.

Einat Admony is chef and owner of Balaboosta, Bar Bolonat, Taïm, and Kish-Kash in New York City, and author of *Balaboosta: Bold Mediterranean Recipes to Feed the People You Love*. Einat was born in Israel to a Yemenite father and a Persian mother.

José Andrés, named one of *Time*'s "100 Most Influential People" and Outstanding Chef by the James Beard Foundation, is an internationally recognized culinary innovator, author, educator, television personality, humanitarian, and chef/owner of ThinkFoodGroup. A pioneer of Spanish tapas in the United States, he is known for his avant-garde cuisine and his award-winning group of 27 restaurants throughout the country and beyond. His innovative minibar by José Andrés earned two Michelin stars in 2016 and with that, José is the only chef globally that has both a Michelin two-star restaurant and four Bib Gourmands. José's work has earned numerous awards, including the 2015 National Humanities Medal, and he is one of the 12 distinguished recipients of the award from the National Endowment for the Humanities.

Dominique Ansel is a James Beard Award–winning pastry chef and owner of eponymous bakeries in New York, Tokyo, and London, with a forthcoming restaurant opening in Los Angeles in the fall of 2017. He has created some of the most fêted pastries in the world, including the Cronut®, named one of *TIME* magazine's "25 Best Inventions of 2013." For his prolific creativity, he was named the World's Best Pastry Chef in 2017 by the World's 50 Best Restaurants awards. *Food & Wine* has called him a "Culinary Van Gogh" while the *New York Post* coined him "the Willy Wonka of New York." He was also named *Business Insider*'s "Most Innovative People Under 40," one of *Crain*'s "40 under 40," and was bestowed the prestigious l'Ordre du Mérite Agricole, France's second-highest honor. Prior to opening his own shop, Dominique served as the executive pastry chef for restaurant DANIEL, when the team earned its coveted third Michelin star and a four-star review from the *New York Times*.

A native of Dublin, Ireland, **Cathal Armstrong** is the chef and owner of Restaurant Eve, the flagship among his chain of Alexandria, Virginia, establishments, where he balances a commitment to locally sourced, fresh ingredients with a fine-dining experience. He has been recognized by the James Beard Foundation with nominations for Best Chef, Mid-Atlantic in 2011, 2012, and 2013. *Food & Wine* included him among their "10 Best New Chefs" in 2006, and their "50 Hall of Fame Best New Chefs." He has also been recognized for his contributions to the local food movement and for his work to preserve and protect the environment. Under President Obama's Winning the Future initiative, the White House honored him as a "Champion of Change." He is author of *My Irish Table: Recipes from the Homeland and Restaurant Eve*.

Reem Assil is the chef and founder of Reem's in Oakland, California. Reem's was founded with a passion for the flavors of Arab street-corner bakeries and the vibrant communities where they're located. Growing up in a Palestinian-Syrian household, Reem was surrounded by the aromas and tastes of food from her homeland and the connections they evoked of her heritage, family, and community. Before dedicating herself to a culinary career, Reem worked for a decade as a community and labor organizer, and brings the warmth of community to all her events. In 2017, she graduated from La Cocina, a competitive food business incubator program focusing on immigrant women.

Nick Balla was born in Michigan, but it was his time living in Budapest as an adolescent that left a lasting culinary mark. After graduating from the CIA Hyde Park, Nick spent extensive time in Japan, where he further learned precision and craftsmanship, before moving to San Francisco, California. In the Bay Area, he ran the kitchen at O Izakaya and Nombe, before returning to the flavors of Central Europe at Bar Tartine. There, Nick and co-chef Cortney Burns created a new type of dining in the city, one that transcended geography and celebrated the larder. Together, they published a James Beard Award–winning book, *Bar Tartine: Techniques & Recipes* (Chronicle Books, November 2014). In June 2017, Nick opened Duna, a Central European-inspired fast-casual eatery in the heart of San Francisco's Mission district.

Hailed as "the guru of Persian cuisine" by the *Washington Post*, **Najmieh Batmanglij** has spent the past 37 years cooking, traveling, teaching, and adapting authentic Persian recipes to tastes and techniques in the US. She is author of four award-winning cookbooks, most recently *Joon: Persian Cooking Made Simple*. Her seminal cookbook, *Food of Life: Ancient Persian and Modern Iranian Cooking and Ceremonies*, was called "the definitive book on Iranian cooking" by the *Los Angeles Times*. Najmieh is a member of Les Dames d'Escoffier and lives in Washington, DC.

Tsiona Bellete left Ethiopia in 1982 to pursue higher education in the US. After 30 years, living, studying to earn a Master's Degree in Pharmaceutical Sciences, and working, she discovered her passion for cooking. Five years ago, she opened Sheba Restaurant in Rockville, Maryland, followed by Tsiona Foods, a small-batch gourmet Ethiopian food company that brings Ethiopian flair to the American market.

Emma Bengtsson grew up in Falkenberg, Sweden, and became interested in the culinary arts at a young age, thanks to her grandmother. Emma trained at Stockholm's Hotel and Restaurant School and went on to work at Edsbacka Krog, where she discovered her love of pastry. After working in some of Sweden's top kitchens, including Restaurant Prinsen and Operakällaren, Emma joined Aquavit in 2010 as pastry chef. In Spring 2014, she became executive chef, garnering a second Michelin star for Aquavit, making her the second female chef in the US to run a two-star kitchen, and the first ever Swedish female chef to do so. She lives in New York.

Rawia Bishara is chef and co-owner of Tanoreen restaurant in Bay Ridge, Brooklyn. She emigrated from her hometown of Nazareth to New York 40 years ago. She is the author of *Olives, Lemons & Za'atar*, published in 2014. Her second cookbook will be released in 2018.

April Bloomfield is executive chef and co-owner of The Spotted Pig, The Breslin Bar & Dining Room, The John Dory Oyster Bar, Tosca Cafe, Salvation Taco, White Gold Butchers, and most recently, The Hearth & Hound in Los Angeles, California. She won the 2014 James Beard Award for Best Chef, New York City, and was nominated for an Emmy for cohosting the second season of the PBS show *Mind of a Chef*. She is author of *A Girl and Her Pig* and *A Girl and Her Greens*. A native of Birmingham, England, she lives in New York City.

A native of Lyon, France, **Daniel Boulud** is considered one of America's leading culinary authorities and one of the most revered French chefs in New York, his home since 1982. Daniel is chef-owner of 14 restaurants around the world, and is best known for his eponymous, exquisitely refined DANIEL on Manhattan's Upper East Side. Daniel is also the author of nine cookbooks and the recipient of numerous awards, including the James Beard Foundation's Outstanding Chef and Outstanding Restaurateur. He has been a generous supporter

and co-president of Citymeals-on-Wheels for more than two decades, and is chairman of the ment'or BKB foundation.

Naji Boustany is executive chef and operations director at Manousheh, a Lebanese eatery in New York City. He was a contestant on the Food Network's *Chopped* in 2017. He was born in Beirut, Lebanon, and his family is from Deir al Qamar, in the al Chouf Mountains. He first learned to cook in his mother's kitchen, growing up to manage a local farmers' market, before overseeing the kitchen of Tawlet Souk el Tayeb, a farm-to-table restaurant in Beirut. He is co-founder of FERN, a Lebanese NGO that works to transform Beirut's restaurants into waste-free establishments.

Marco Canora is an Italian-American chef, restaurateur, and author of three cookbooks. His restaurant, Hearth, in New York's East Village, quickly became a culinary destination, even before its reinvention in 2016. Brodo kicked off America's bone broth craze and continues to be an industry leader. His recent venture, Zadie's Oyster Room, opened in 2016, is an ode to turn-of-the-century oyster houses. In 2017, Marco won the James Beard Award for Best Chef, New York. His appreciation for delicious food has been a part of him since his childhood in upstate New York, where he enjoyed the freshest herbs and vegetables from the garden and cooked with his mother for hours on end. When he's not in the kitchen, Marco enjoys time with his family in Martha's Vineyard.

Carla Capalbo is a freelance journalist, photographer, and author of fourteen books on food and wine. Her latest book *Tasting Georgia: A Food and Wine Journey in the Caucasus* was published in 2017. *Collio: Fine Wines and Foods from Italy's Northeast* won a prestigious André Simon Award; and her photography has won several awards, including from the IACP's Culinary Trust. She is closely linked to Slow Food, and a member of the Guild of Food Writers and Circle of Wine Writers.

Joanne Chang was an honors graduate of Harvard College with a degree in Applied Mathematics and Economics, when she left a career as a management consultant to enter the world of professional cooking. She is the chef and co-owner of Flour Bakery + Café, with seven locations in the Boston area, and Myers + Chang. She is the winner of the James Beard Award for Outstanding Baker, as well as the author of *Flour: Spectacular Recipes from Boston's Flour Bakery + Cafe; Flour, too: Indispensable Recipes for the Café's Most Loved Sweets & Savories; Baking with Less Sugar;* and *Myers + Chang at Home: Recipes from the Beloved Boston Eatery*. She is currently working on her fifth book, *Pastry Love*.

Mei Chau was born into a large Chinese family in Malaysia, which is known for its colorful, mixed culture, dating back to the time when the first West-East trade began. She is the tenth child in her family and grew up in a small fishing village famous for its stretch of white sandy beaches, and for being the home of the giant turtle. She opened her first restaurant, Franklin Station Café, a French/Malaysian bistro in New York City's Tribeca neighborhood, in 1993. Her second restaurant, Aux Epices, was opened in 2013 in Chinatown.

Lauryn Chun is the author of *The Kimchi Cookbook: 60 Traditional and Modern Ways to Make and Eat Kimchi* (2012) and the founder of Mother-in-Law's Kimchi, the first line of artisanal kimchi and gochujang sauces sold in natural and specialty retailers nationally. She was inspired by the beauty of Korea's handcrafted tradition of kimchi as a fine food that belongs in the ranks of fine wine, cheese, and beer traditions. Mother-in-Law's Kimchi is based on an original recipe from her mother's 29-year-old restaurant, Jang Mo Jip (Mother-in-Law's House) in California. Mother-in-Law's Kimchi has received unprecedented press accolades in the *New York Times*, *Wall Street Journal*, *Ad Week*, *O the Oprah Magazine*, WNYC, *USA Today*, *Rachael Ray Every Day*, *Men's Health*, *Tasting Table*, and more, and has been featured on MSNBC and the Cooking Channel's *FoodCrafters*. Lauryn lives in Brooklyn, New York.

Ejhadji Cisse and **Cheikh Cisse** are the owners and executive chefs of Ponty Bistro in New York City. The cousins moved to the United States from Senegal in 1995. They entered the restaurant business fourteen years ago and, between them, have worked for internationally renowned chefs, such as Daniel Boulud at DANIEL, Jean-Georges Vongerichten at Vong and Mercer Kitchen, and others. Ponty Bistro fulfilled their dream to own a restaurant, and features a three-star menu of unique African and French cuisine.

A native of St. Lucia, **Nina Compton** is chef and owner of Compère Lapin in New Orleans, which received a rave review in the *New York Times*, and was listed in the top 10 of *Playboy*'s "Best New Bars in America, 2016," and named Best New Restaurant by *New Orleans Magazine* and *Times-Picayune*. In 2017, she was a finalist for a James Beard Award for Best Chef, South, and *Food & Wine* named her as one of their "Best New Chefs in America." In addition to the success of her first restaurant, Nina is also currently the culinary ambassador of St. Lucia.

Recognized as one of the mothers of modern food culture, **Ariane Daguin** is the founder, owner, and CEO of D'Artagnan, the leading purveyor of sustainable, humanely-raised meats, charcuterie, foie gras, and mushrooms in the United States. Since D'Artagnan's founding in 1985, Ariane has emerged as a culinary innovator among America's top chefs, partnering with small family farms dedicated to natural production of the finest quality and healthiest meat, game, and poultry. A pioneer in the farm-to-table movement, Ariane introduced the first organic, free-range chicken years before the USDA allowed the word "organic" on the label. Ariane continues to influence and inspire the food industry by introducing new products, creating new animal breeds, and implementing innovative and ecologically responsible methods of production.

Jesus Delgado is executive chef of Tanta in Chicago, a collaboration with well-known South American Chef Gastón Acurio. Jesus was born and raised in Peru, one of the world's most diverse and eclectic food cultures. He worked at number of Chinese- and Japanese-influenced restaurants in Lima, before landing at Acurio's La Mar Cebicheria in 2007 as a line cook. By 2011, Jesus had worked his way up and excelled in the role of ceviche chef, creating a diverse menu of traditional and unexpected fresh fish dishes and other cold plates, cementing his reputation for showcasing Peruvian seafood in distinctive and unexpected ways. He moved to Chicago, Illinois in 2013 to lead Tanta's kitchen.

Moussa Doulaeh is executive chef and co-owner of Afro Deli, a fusion restaurant with locations in St. Paul, and Minneapolis, Minnesota. At Afro Deli, he combines the cuisine of his native East Africa, with the many flavors learned from his formal culinary training in top Canadian and American kitchens, or gathered from cooking with friends from around the world. In April 2017, Afro Deli initiated the Dine Out for Somalia campaign, a fundraiser with 50 participating restaurants, to support famine relief efforts.

Ron Duprat is best known from Bravo TV's *Top Chef*, *Iron Chef America*, and *Bar Rescue*. His cuisine combines the rich flavors of his Caribbean heritage with French accents. Duprat has been featured on *The View*, *BET*, *Gourmet*, *Elle*, *Bon Appetit*, *Essence*, the *Root*, *O the Oprah Magazine*, and was one of *Ebony*'s "Top Chefs, 2015." The *Huffington Post* recognized him as one of "10 Black Chefs that are Changing the Food World." Ron is a member of the U.S. State Department's Chef Corps for Diplomatic Culinary Partnership, and has prepared meals for President and First Lady Obama, Jay Z and Beyoncé, Usher, and many more. He's affiliated with several major causes, including fighting childhood obesity, Michelle Obama's "Let's Move" campaign, No Hungry Kids, The Black Culinarian Alliance (BCA), The Word and Actions, World Central Kitchen, and Clean Cook Stove.

Laila El-Haddad is a Maryland-based freelance journalist, documentarian, and cookbook author. She is the author of *The Gaza Kitchen: A Palestinian Culinary Journey*. She frequently writes on the intersection of food and politics and she is currently working on a book about the history of Islam in America, as told through food.

Paulina Farro is a food writer, blogger, and illustrator eating her way around the world. She infuses her recipes with the foods she discovers on her travels, writing about them for her blog *Potato Chips are Not Dinner*, which is a finalist in the 2017 *Saveur* blog awards. As a second-generation immigrant, it is her passion to bring Filipino food to the forefront of the culinary world. When her mother came to the United States from the Philippines, she was told to only speak English and do whatever she could to fit into American culture, erasing many of her recipes and traditions. Paulina strives to bring those back through her writing, illustrations, and recipes.

Born in Hong Kong, **Lina Fat** was a pharmacist in Sacramento, California, for many years, before joining her husband's family's restaurant business in 1974. Her passion for cooking and menu creation landed her the role of head chef when the Fat Family Restaurant Group expanded, with the opening of their second restaurant, China Camp, in 1974, followed by Fat City Bar & Café in 1976. Today, Lina wears several hats in the Fat Family Restaurant Group. She is vice president of culinary research and development, and oversees four restaurants and a catering division. She continues to play an active role in the community, promoting cultural diversity throughout the Sacramento area.

Ivan Garcia is chef and owner of Mesa Coyoacan, Zona Rosa, and Guadalupe Inn in Brooklyn. He was born and raised in the Coyoacan neighborhood of Mexico City and moved to New York in 2000, honing his personal style in some of the city's top restaurants. Ivan holds great reverence for authentic Mexican dishes. His style celebrates his heritage and highlights the diverse flavors and ingredients ubiquitous in Mexican cuisine.

Born in Austria, **Markus Glocker** grew up working in the family hotels, where his appreciation for the culinary arts became a passion. In 2014, Markus opened Bâtard, New York, with restaurateur Drew Nieporent and managing partner John Winterman. His modern European cuisine earned three stars from *New York Magazine,* three stars from the *New York Times,* and a Michelin star, among other stellar reviews. In May 2015, Bâtard was awarded Best New Restaurant in America by the James Beard Foundation.

Salma Hage is a James Beard Award winner and best-selling author of two Middle Eastern cookbooks. Her cookbook *The Lebanese Kitchen* is considered the definitive book on Lebanese home cooking. Growing up in Mazarat Tiffah (Apple Hamlet), in the mountains of the Kadisha Valley in North Lebanon, she learned to cook from her mother, mother-in-law, and sisters-in-law. Having helped bring up her nine brothers and two sisters, she grew up cooking for the whole family. She has pursued this love for cooking throughout her life, working for many years as a professional cook.

Nadia Hassani is the author of the book and blog, *Spoonfuls of Germany: German Regional Cuisine,* and the blog, *Green Card Gardener.* She is a copywriter, editor, and translator. She was born in Germany to a German mother and a Tunisian father, and immigrated to the United States as an adult in the late 1990s. In her garden in rural Pennsylvania, she grows many fruits and vegetables for the dishes of her mixed heritage.

Colombian-born **Ingrid Hoffmann** developed a love for cooking as a child, learning from her mother, a Cordon Bleu–trained chef. As a teenager, she worked in her mom's catering business.

Upon moving to Miami, they opened a restaurant together. As host of *Top Chef Estrellas* on Telemundo, *Delicioso* on Univision, and *Simply Delicioso* on the Cooking Channel, Ingrid has become a leading Latin authority on cooking and lifestyle, and her Delicioso brand has become one of the most recognizable, trusted, and entertaining food brands for Hispanic America. Find her at www.ingridhoffmann.com.

Didem Hosgel was raised in a traditional Turkish family where cooking from scratch and preparing food for family members was an ongoing and cherished practice. After moving to the US in 2001, Didem set her roots in Boston and began working for Chef Ana Sortun at the famed Oleana Restaurant in Cambridge, Massachusetts. After many years at Oleana, she became chef de cuisine at Sofra Bakery, a Middle Eastern-inspired bakery and cafe. At Sofra, she creates innovative new dishes using fresh, local ingredients, while still honoring her Turkish roots.

Nadia Hubbi is a food stylist, photographer, blogger, and founder of Sweet Pillar, a Modern Middle Eastern Food company specializing in dips, cookies, and confectionary. She writes about modern and traditional dishes handed down from her Syrian family on her blog *Sweet Pillar FOOD.* She was raised in New Jersey and currently resides in Southern California with her family.

Anita Jaisinghani is of Sindhi descent, and was born and raised in Gujarat, India. She came to the US in the 1990s by way of Canada. She owned and operated Indika restaurant in Houston, Texas, for 16 years and is now the chef and owner of Pondicheri, an India-inspired café focusing on street and home cooking with two locations in New York City and Houston, Texas.

Katrina Jazayeri is co-owner, with partner chef Joshua Lewin, of Juliet, named one of *Bon Appetit*'s "50 Best New Restaurants in America." Born in Queens, New York, to an Iranian father and an American mother who were brought together by food, she saw firsthand its power to create relationships, memories, and lasting connections. At 26 years old, Katrina was awarded one of 19 *Eater* Young Guns Awards in 2016, and was named one of *Zagat*'s "30 under 30" in 2014. Juliet is Boston's first tip-free restaurant. Katrina and Josh apply their commitment to social justice to their business to create a supportive work environment, featuring a profit-sharing model in favor of the traditional restaurant wage structure.

Deana Kabakibi is co–content creator of *Sweet Pillar FOOD.* She gave up a career as a lawyer to follow her passion for cooking and baking, and hasn't looked back. She is Syrian, by way of New York, and currently lives in Los Angeles.

Zareen Khan is a chef, cooking instructor, and restaurateur of Pakistani heritage. She learned the art of cooking from her mother, aunts, and sister. After teaching cooking classes and launching a successful catering business in the Bay Area, she opened Zareen's Restaurant in Mountain View, California, in 2010, to showcase the foods of Karachi, Bombay, and Punjab. She opened a second location in Palo Alto in 2016. In 2017, Zareen's Mountain View was included in the *Michelin Guide*. Zareen is a member of the Farm-to-Consumer Legal Defense Fund, Weston A. Price Foundation, and Farm Sanctuary.

Thomas Kim is chef and owner of Rabbit Hole Restaurant in Minneapolis. He is Korean-American, born and raised in Los Angeles. He grew up eating Korean food, but his culinary background is in fine-dining Japanese cuisine. After work, he frequently ate at local taquerias and burger stands, so he and his wife set out to create a restaurant that honors all of those influences and reflects the current American culinary landscape.

Josh Ku and **Trigg Brown** met at a cookout and bonded over Taiwanese food. Eating and cooking Taiwanese food became a regular activity that elucidated the lack of Taiwanese representation in the NYC culinary landscape. Their restaurant, Win Son, in Williamsburg, Brooklyn, communicates their version of Taiwanese food, and raises awareness for the nuanced and complex nature of Taiwanese food, culture, politics, and history.

Ryan Lachaine is executive chef and co-owner of Riel, in Houston, Texas. His first culinary education began at the apron strings of his Ukrainian mother and grandmother in his family home in Manitoba, Canada. He trained under Chef Bryan Caswell at Stella Sola, before staging at some of the country's top restaurants, earning him an induction into *Eater's* 2013 Class of Young Guns. He named Riel after Louis Riel, the founder of Manitoba and leader of the Métis community and the movement to preserve the group's native lands, culture, and languages. Ryan chose Riel to represent his own Canadian heritage and the many cultures that Riel sought to bring together, something Ryan does on the plates of his restaurant.

Arriving in California from Marrakesh in 1985 to study, a homesick **Mourad Lahlou** began to channel his mother and aunts as they prepared traditional Moroccan dishes at home. He started to cook for himself, then for friends. He completed a master's degree in macroeconomics, but the lure of the kitchen pulled him from his doctorate, and he opened his first restaurant, in San Rafael, California, in 1997. He then opened the modern Aziza, named after his mother, in San Francisco in 2001. In 2009, he won *Iron Chef America* by the largest margin in the history of the show. And in 2010, Aziza became the first Moroccan restaurant to receive a Michelin star. He is the author of *Mourad: New Moroccan*.

Anita Lo is a first-generation Chinese-American chef and restaurateur, formerly of the highly acclaimed Annisa restaurant in New York City. She is the author of *Cooking without Borders*. Her second cookbook will be published in the fall of 2018.

Maria Loi is a Greek chef, restaurateur, cookbook author, TV personality, and philanthropist based in New York City, where she runs her acclaimed restaurant, Loi Estiatorio. She was elected global ambassador of Greek gastronomy by the Chef's Club of Greece, and has founded a range of food products, including Loi Pasta, Loi Dips, and soon, Loi Yogurt, sold by Whole Foods Markets in Manhattan. Maria's mission in life is to change the world, one healthy Greek bite at a time!

Serge Madikians is chef/owner of Serevan in the Hudson Valley, New York. After a childhood in pre-revolutionary Tehran, he came to the US for his undergraduate studies in California and graduate school at the New School in New York, where he studied public policy and economics. While working for the City of New York, he took night classes at the International Culinary Center, going on to work with renowned chefs Jean-George Vongerichten and David Bouley. After opening his own restaurant in 2005, he was named Best Chef in the Hudson Valley by *Hudson Valley Magazine* and was a semifinalist for the James Beard Awards' Best Chef in the Northeast, both for two years running. The cuisine at Serevan celebrates the abundance of the Hudson Valley and Serevan's own gardens, through the prism of Iranian and Iranian-Armenian flavor spectrums and cultural heritage.

Alicia Maher is the author of *Delicious El Salvador*, which won Gourmand's Best First Cookbook award in 2014. She was born and raised in El Salvador and has made California her home since 1986. She teaches cooking classes privately, and at Whole Foods Markets in Los Angeles. Known as "El Salvador's Culinary Ambassador," she will soon launch the Spanish edition of *Delicious El Salvador*, and is working on her second Salvadoran cookbook. She lives in California with her husband, Joseph Maher, and their three sons.

A seven-time Grammy winner, Emmy winner, humanitarian, singer, songwriter, and producer, **Ziggy Marley** has released twelve albums to much critical acclaim. His early immersion in music came at age ten when he sat in on recording sessions with his father, Bob Marley. Ziggy also recently released his debut children's book *I Love You Too*, a multicultural picture book based on one of Ziggy's most beloved songs of the same title from his Grammy Award–winning album *Family Time*. His latest book is the *Ziggy Marley and Family Cookbook*. He is originally from Jamaica and lives in California.

Cristina Martinez crossed the desert to come and make a career in the United States. As an undocumented female chef and restaurateur, she challenges gender stereotypes and raises awareness for the plight of undocumented workers through her restaurant, El Compadre, in Philadelphia, Pennsylvania. In 2016, *Bon Appétit* named her first restaurant, South Philly Barbacoa (now closed), in the top 10 of their "Best New Restaurants in America." Cristina was born into a family of *barbacoteros* in Capulhuac, Mexico, and was raised cooking in the family business. She lives in Philadelphia with her husband, Benjamin.

Born in the Sonoran border town of Agua Prieta, **Zarela Martinez** is a renowned cultural interpreter between Mexico and the United States through the medium of food. For 23 years her eponymous restaurant, Zarela, set standards of authenticity among New York Mexican restaurants. A sought-after speaker and consultant, she also wrote the pioneering cookbooks *Food from My Heart*, *The Food and Life of Oaxaca*, and *Zarela's Veracruz*, the last published in conjunction with her public television series *¡Zarela! La Cocina Veracruzana*. Her website www.zarela.com is an invaluable resource for lovers of Mexican food and culture, and her how-to videos on basic Mexican cooking techniques and flavor principles featured on YouTube are fun and informative.

Barbara Abdeni Massaad is a food writer, TV host, and cookbook author. Born in Beirut, Lebanon, she moved to Florida at a young age, gaining her first culinary experience helping her father in their family-owned Lebanese restaurant, Kebabs and Things. She went on to train with renowned chefs at Lebanese, Italian, and French restaurants. Her first cookbook, *Man'oushé: Inside the Lebanese Street-Corner Bakery*, won The Lebanese Academy of Gastronomy Award in 2009. Her book *Soup for Syria: Recipes to Celebrate Our Shared Humanity* gathered recipes from prominent chefs to help raise funds for food and medical relief efforts for Syrian refugees. Her latest book, *Mouneh: Preserving Foods for the Lebanese Pantry* (Interlink, 2017) continues her quest to discover and preserve Lebanese culinary heritage. She is a founding member of Slow Food Beirut and a member of Les Ambassadeurs du Pain.

Ignacio Mattos is co-owner and chef of Estela, Café Altro Paradiso, and Flora Bar at the Met Breuer in New York. He was born in Uruguay and learned to cook in the kitchens of grilling master Francis Mallman and Slow Food legend Alice Waters. Per *New York Times* critic Pete Wells: "[Ignacio's] dishes are original and, in their way, simple, and it's that combination that makes you want to give in to them." In 2017, Ignacio received his third nomination for the James Beard Award for Best Chef, New York. Ignacio cooks food that is comforting and memorable, reflecting his varied experiences and the cultures of New York City, the city he now calls home.

Roni Mazumdar is a New York–based restaurateur. Growing up in Kolkata, India, food played a central role in his household. In 2011, he opened the Masalawala, which he runs with his father. Its success led Roni to open a second location in 2016, followed shortly by Rahi, a modern Indian restaurant named *Zagat*'s hottest new restaurant in 2017; and recently, Unico, a globally-influenced fast-casual restaurant in Long Island City, named in *New York Magazine*'s "Best New Cheap Eats, 2017," and *Eater*'s "Hottest Restaurants in Queens." He has used his success to benefit his community, establishing a scholarship program in West Bengal, India; as well as working to empower victims of domestic abuse and sex trafficking in New York City; and staffing and training students from LaGuardia Community

College's Food Service Management Program.

Monica Meehan has spent her life exploring her diverse roots and passion for food, travel, and culture. Raised in Canada by her Austrian mother and British father, she resided in London for over a decade, before relocating to New York City, where she continues a successful career in publishing. Her internationally celebrated cookbook, *The Viennese Kitchen*, is rich with her family's affluent history and sumptuous recipes, against the breathtaking backdrop of turn-of-the-century Vienna.

Claus Meyer is the initiator of the New Nordic Cuisine movement, co-founder of the Nordic Food Lab, and the now legendary Noma. Claus has hosted several Danish and international cooking shows and written numerous cookbooks. Believing in food as a driver for social change, he established the Melting Pot Foundation in 2010, which initiated a cooking school project in Danish state prisons; and a cooking school in La Paz, Bolivia, which provides culinary education to impoverished Bolivians and serves as a fine-dining restaurant, GUSTU. This summer, Claus's newest social project is the Brownsville Community Culinary Center, a culinary school, cafeteria, bakery, and community center. In 2016 he opened Agern and the Great Northern Food Hall in Grand Central Terminal, bringing the culinary concepts, flavors, and ideas rooted in the history and landscapes of Nordic countries to New York City.

Bonnie Morales (née Frumkin) grew up in Chicago in a large Belarusian family. She trained at the Culinary Institute of America, honing her skills in Michelin-starred restaurants, including Tru, where she met her future husband and business partner, Israel Morales. In 2014, the Morales' opened Kachka, in Portland, Oregon. Kachka has received accolades from *Bon Appétit*, the *Wall Street Journal*, the *New York Times*, *Elle*, and *Food & Wine*. *Eater National* included Kachka in their "Best Restaurants in America" in 2015 and 2016. Bonnie was named one of *Tasting Table*'s "New Originals," and a "Next Generation Chef" by *Bon Appétit* in 2017. The restaurant recently launched a craft spirits line, and the Morales' first cookbook, *Kachka: A Return to Russian Cooking* (Flatiron Books), was published in November 2017.

Dalia Mortada is an American journalist of Syrian heritage. She has spent recent years telling stories of Syrians now in the Diaspora through the lens of food, for her special project *Savoring Syria*. She also hosts dining events for Syrians and their new communities in cities throughout the US and Europe, as a way to break down barriers by breaking bread. She lives in Virginia.

Joan Nathan is author of eleven cookbooks, including her latest work, *King Solomon's Table: A Culinary Exploration of Jewish Cooking from around the World*, released in April 2017 by Alfred P. Knopf. Joan has received numerous awards for her cookbooks, including multiple James Beard Awards and accolades from the International Association of Culinary Professionals. She is a regular contributor to the *New York Times* and *Tablet* magazine.

Hari Nayak is a chef, cookbook author, restaurateur, and consultant born in Udupi, a small town in South India famous for vegetarian cooking. He has authored six cookbooks and is recognized as a pioneer of modern Indian cuisine and for his vision is to bring Indian culture and cuisine to the forefront of the global culinary map. He lives in New Jersey.

Enrique Olvera is a leader of Mexico's new gastronomy, fueled by a constant exploration of Mexico's ingredients and culinary history. In 2000, at the age of 24, he opened the globally-recognized restaurant, Pujol, in Mexico City. He now also owns four outposts of Eno in Mexico City; Manta, in Los Cabos; and Cosme and Atla in New York City. He is author of *Mexico from the Inside Out*. Over time, he has created a cosmopolitan cuisine that is modern in approach but anchored by Mexican tradition. He prefers not to categorize his dishes. Instead, it is flavor that drives and guides him. He divides his time between New York and Mexico City.

Ana Patuleia Ortins is a culinary instructor and chef, and author of two cookbooks, *Portuguese Homestyle Cooking* and *Authentic Portuguese Cooking*. She is a first-generation descendant of Portuguese immigrants from the small town of Galveias in the Alto Alentejo province of Portugal. She lives in Massachusetts.

Ana Sofía Peláez is a Miami-based food writer covering the spectrum of Latin American cuisine on her blog, *Hungry Sofia*. The site has been featured by *InStyle* and *Food 52*, and was nominated by *Saveur* as one of the best regional cuisine blogs of 2012. Her work has appeared in *Smithsonian Journeys* magazine and NBCNews.com, among other national outlets. Her first cookbook, *The Cuban Table* (St. Martin's Press) was nominated for a James Beard Award in 2015.

Charles Phan is the inventor of modern Vietnamese cuisine in America and executive chef and owner of the Slanted Door family of restaurants. Born in Da Lat, Vietnam, the Phan family relocated just before the fall of Saigon in 1975, spending two years in Guam before settling in San Francisco. Charles opened his first restaurant, The Slanted Door, in 1995. In 2014, the restaurant was named Outstanding Restaurant by the James Beard Foundation. His current restaurants in San Francisco are Out the Door, OTD, and Hard Water. Upcoming projects are Rice and Bones at Wurster Hall UC Berkeley, and The Slanted Door in other urban areas. Charles has been featured on Food Network's *Iron Chef America* and Mark Bittman's *How to Cook Everything*. In 2004, he won the James Beard Foundation's Best Chef, California. He is author of two cookbooks, *Vietnamese Home Cooking*, and *The Slanted Door*, both winning IACP cookbook awards. He is a leader in the San

Francisco food community and has participated in countless charitable events.

Born and raised in Bangkok, Thailand, **Leela Punyaratabandhu** came to the United States for school. She writes about Thai food on her award-winning website, *She Simmers*, and has authored two books: *Bangkok: Recipes and Stories from the Heart of Thailand* and *Simple Thai Food: Classic Recipes from the Thai Home Kitchen*. Leela has been named one of the 100 Greatest Home Cooks of All Time by *Epicurious*. She splits her time between Chicago and Bangkok.

Hanif Sadr was born in Paris, France, and raised in Tehran, Iran. He is chef and co-founder of Komaaj, a Northern Iranian pop-up restaurant and catering company based in Berkeley, California.

Aarón Sánchez is an award-winning Mexican-American chef and TV personality. He is the chef and owner of Johnny Sánchez, with locations in New Orleans and Baltimore, and a judge on FOX's hit culinary competition series *Masterchef*. He co-starred on Food Network's *Chopped* and *Chopped Junior*, and is the author of two cookbooks. An active philanthropist, Aarón launched the Aarón Sánchez Scholarship Fund, enabling aspiring chefs from the Latin-American community to attend culinary school. Aarón is passionate about preserving his family's legacy through food and encouraging diversity in the kitchen.

Samantha Seneviratne is an author and food stylist. Her first cookbook, *The New Sugar and Spice*, was nominated for a 2016 James Beard Award. She's also the author of *Gluten Free For Good* and a contributor to various food media outlets including the *New York Times* and *Martha Stewart*. She is currently focusing on a new book and a new baby in Brooklyn.

Born in Hilo, Hawaii, **Sheldon Simeon** acquired his love for cooking from his Filipino parents. Trained at the Culinary Institute of the Pacific and Maui Culinary Academy, he competed in the 10th and 14th seasons of Bravo Network's *Top Chef: Seattle* and *Charleston* as a finalist, winning "Fan Favorite" both times. After serving as the executive chef at Maui's Mala Wailea, MiGRANT, and Star Noodle, he was nominated for two James Beard Awards: Rising Star Chef of the Year, and Best New Restaurant, and was named *Food & Wine*'s People's Best New Chef for the Pacific & Northwest in 2014. He is chef and owner of Tin Roof in Kahului, Maui, serving up his playful take on classic local dishes.

David SooHoo was born into the restaurant life. His father, newly arrived in Sacramento from Canton, China, opened many old-style Cantonese restaurants. In 1985, Chef SooHoo and his family opened the modern and lavish 5-star restaurant Chinois East-West. He was the first Sacramento chef invited to cook and teach at the James Beard House in New York.

Ana Sortun graduated from La Varenne Ecole de Cuisine de Paris and opened her restaurant, Oleana, in 2001, immediately drawing rave reviews from the *New York Times*. She was named Best Chef in the Northeast by the James Beard Foundation in 2005, and went on to open Sofra Bakery and Café. She is the author of *Spice: Flavors of the Eastern Mediterranean* and, most recently, *Soframiz: Vibrant Middle Eastern Recipes from Sofra Bakery and Café* (with Maura Kilpatrick).

Cara Stadler is the chef and owner of Tao Yuan Restaurant and Bao Bao Dumpling House in Brunswick and Portland, Maine. Her cooking earned her a James Beard Award nomination in the category of Rising Star Chef, and *Food & Wine* named her Best New Chef in 2014. She is from Harvard, Massachusetts, and has lived in Paris, Philadelphia, Berkeley, Shanghai, Singapore, and Beijing. Her food is the culmination of her heritage and travels.

Curtis Stone is a chef, restaurateur, media personality, businessman, and *New York Times* best-selling author. He gained his twelve years' culinary training in his native Australia, and in Europe, eight years of which were under renowned chef Marco Pierre White. He currently lives in Los Angeles, California, where he debuted his first solo restaurant, Maude, in Beverly Hills, and partnered with his brother Luke to open Gwen Butcher Shop & Restaurant in Hollywood.

John Sugimura is executive chef, concept-brand director, and partner at PinKU Japanese Street Food in Minneapolis, Minnesota. He is a second-generation Japanese-American professionally trained sushi chef, whose life-long love of sushi blossomed during time spent in Osaka and Kyoto, Japan. Eating John's cuisine is like eating in his grandmother's restaurant in the 1930s. It is the ultimate expression of flavors, colors, and cooking methods, coming together in an authentic experience that is one of a kind.

Born in Indonesia to Indonesian-Chinese parents and raised in Singapore, **Pat Tanumihardja** credits her eclectic culinary aptitude and global outlook to her multicultural background. Pat has been a food and lifestyle writer for over a decade. Her cookbooks include *Farm to Table Asian Secrets: Vegan and Vegetarian Full-Flavored Recipes for Every Season* and *The Asian Grandmothers Cookbook*. She lives in Springfield, Virginia, with her husband and son. Find Pat on Twitter: @PicklesandTea, Instagram: @Pickles.and.Tea, and on the web: SmithsonianAPA.org/PicklesandTea.

Tunde Wey is a Nigerian cook and writer. He moved to the United States at 16. Since 2016, he has been traveling across the country with his pop-up dinner series, Blackness in America, which explores race in America from the Black perspective, through food and discussion. You can read more about his projects at FromLagos.com. He currently resides in New Orleans.

Beloved television host, cookbook author, restaurateur, and certified master chef **Martin Yan** has dedicated his life to promoting Chinese cuisine. Born in Guangzhou in Southern China, Martin was first inspired by his mother in the tiny kitchen of their family restaurant. Since 1982, he has hosted the hugely popular PBS cooking show, *Yan Can Cook*, which has been broadcast in 50 countries and has won numerous awards. He is also host of *Martin Yan, Quick & Easy*; *Martin Yan's Chinatowns*; and *Martin Yan's Hidden China*. He has written more than two dozen cookbooks, owns three restaurants, and has appeared as a guest judge on *Iron Chef America*, *Top Chef*, and *Hell's Kitchen*. He lives in California.

PHOTO CREDITS

Unless noted below, food photography by Ricarius Photography, www.ricariusphotography.com.

Appetizers

p. 16 Araceli Paz

p. 17 Fiamma Piacentini

p. 18 Galdones Photography

p. 19 Mistey Nguyen

p. 20 Signe Birck

p. 21 Rachael Calmas

p. 22 Jung Fitzpatrick
    Photography

p. 24 Saeideh Akbari

p. 25 Phi Tran

Salads

p. 30 Thomas Schauer

p. 31 Melissa Hom

p. 32 Tuukka Koski

p. 33 Daniel Krieger

p. 34 Carly Diaz

p. 35 Carly Diaz

p. 36 Artur Ram

p. 37 Evan Sung

p. 39 Eric Wolfinger

p. 40 Chris Cham

p. 42 Raymond Yazbeck

p. 43 Barbara Abdeni Massaad

Soups

p. 46 Ryan Forbes

p. 48 Mark C. Austin

p. 50 Lorna Stovall

p. 52 Michael Harlan Turkell

p. 53 Michael Harlan Turkell

p. 54 Max Flatow

p. 55 Jack Turkel

p. 56 Alonzo Maciel

p. 60 Marc Ortins

p. 62 Kristin Teig

p. 63 Michael Harlan Turkell

p. 67 Sergii Koval, Dreamstime

Vegetables

p. 70 Thomas Grøndahl

p. 74 Sarah Culver

p. 75 Pat Tanumihardja

p. 79 Carla Capalbo

p. 84 Courtesy of Mage Publishers

p. 85 Courtesy of Mage Publishers

Fish

p. 88 Kii Arens

p. 89 Ryan Robert Miller

p. 92 Ted Axelrod

p. 94 Kristin Teig

p. 97 Ana Sortun

p. 102 Asha Belk

p. 103 Asha Belk

p. 106 Amara Khan

p. 108 Lou Vest

p. 109 Julie Keselman

p. 110 Chef's Eye Photography

p. 111 Julian D. Ramirez

Poultry

p. 115 Anders Schønnemann

p. 120 Laurie Smith

p. 123 Ppy2010ha,
    Dreamstime.com

p. 126 Pacific Dream Photography

Meat

p. 134 Fox

p. 135 Randy Schmidt

p. 136 Scott Suchman

p. 138 Ted Nghiem

p. 140 Courtesy of D'Artagnan

p. 141 Courtesy of D'Artagnan

p. 142 Jenny G. Zhang

p. 143 Patricia Y. Lee

p. 144 Evan Frost

p. 153 Tiverylucky,
    Dreamstime.com

Desserts

p. 156 Ray Kachatorian

p. 157 Jennifer Gomez

p. 158 Stephen Johnson

p. 159 Erin Kunkel

p. 160 Gabriela Herman

p. 162 Samar Hubbi

p. 165 Nadia Hubbi

p. 166 Amy Hou

p. 170 Stacy Horowitz

p. 172 Tara Fisher

p. 174 Danielle Villasana

p. 176 Tatyana Aleksandrova

p. 177 Paulina Farro

p. 178 Ted Rosen

p. 181 Thomas Schauer

p. 182 Thomas Schauer

p. 185 Ana Sofía Peláez

Snacks and Sides

p. 188 Moyo Oyelola

p. 190 Ania Gruca

p. 191 Quentin Bacon

p. 192 Bravo

p. 194 Elsa Hahne

p. 195 Courtesy of Compère
    Lapin

p. 196 Brian Samuels
    Photography

p. 199 Sara Remington

p. 200 Renato D'Agostin

p. 214 David Loftus

p. 219 Julian D. Ramirez

RECIPE CREDITS

Laila El-Haddad: Gazan Hot Tomato and Dill Salad, from *The Gaza Kitchen: A Palestinian Culinary Journey*, published by Just World Books, copyright © Laila El-Haddad, 2016. Reprinted by permission of the author.

Marco Canora: Cranberry Bean Soup with Farro, from *A Good Food Day*, published by Clarkson Potter, an imprint of the Crown Publishing Group, a division of Penguin Random House LLC, copyright © 2014 by Marco Canora. Photography copyright © 2014 by Michael Harlan Turkell. All rights reserved. Reprinted with permission of the author.

Hari Nayak: Lentil and Spinach Soup, from *Café Spice Cookbook*, published by Tuttle Publishing, copyright © Hari Nayak, 2015. Reprinted by permission of the author.

Alicia Maher: Shrimp Soup/Sopa de Camarones, from *Delicious El Salvador: 75 Authentic Recipes for Traditional Salvadoran Cooking*, published by Alicia Maher, copyright © Alicia Maher, 2013. Reprinted by permission.

Ana Patuleia Ortins: Bean Soup, from *Portuguese Homestyle Cooking*, published by Interlink Publishing, copyright © Ana Patuleia Ortins, 2001, 2006, 2008, 2011, 2016. Reprinted by permission.

Joanne Chang: Mama Chang's Hot and Sour Soup, from *Flour Too: Indispensable Recipes for the Café's Most Loved Sweets*, published by Chronicle Books, copyright © Joanne Chang, 2013. Reprinted by permission of the author.

Salma Hage: Lebanese Vegan Moussaka, from *The Middle Eastern Vegetarian Cookbook*, published by Phaidon, copyright © Phaidon Press Limited, 2016. Reprinted by permission.

Patricia Tanumihardja: Turmeric, Zucchini, and Carrot Stir-Fry (Orak Arik), from *Farm to Table Asian Secrets: Vegan and Vegetarian Full-Flavored Recipes for Every Season*, published by Tuttle Publishing, copyright © Patricia Tanumihardja. Reprinted by permission of the author.

Maria Loi: Braised Giant Beans with Spinach, from *The Greek Diet*, published by HarperCollins Publishers, copyright © Maria Loi, 2014. Reprinted by permission.

Najmieh Batmanglij: Pomegranate and Walnut Khoresh, from *Joon: Persian Cooking Made Simple*, published by Mage Publishers, copyright © Najmieh Batmanglij, 2015. Reprinted by permission.

INDEX

ACKNOWLEDGMENTS

To each of the incredible chefs who contributed recipes to this book, and the staff who support you: thank you for generously sharing your stories and your wonderful food, and for continuing to inspire and push the boundaries of American food culture. Your collective voices are a powerful and invaluable force for good.

Thanks, also, to Alice Waters, Anthony Bourdain, Yotam Ottolenghi, David Lebovitz, and Deborah Madison for your encouragement, enthusiasm, and support.

To my father, Michel Moushabeck, and his partner, Hiltrud Schulz, for supporting the book with your time, energy, advice, kitchen skills, and many hours of babysitting.

To the many friends and family who mobilized to offer help, advice, and support, particularly: Ruth Moushabeck, Elizabeth Fournier, Tonya Blundon, Alejandra Holguin, and Samar Moushabeck. And to Hania Moushabeck, Hannah Moushabeck, and Maha Moushabeck for your support from afar.

To Ricky Rodriguez, for your absolutely beautiful photography, calm professionalism and unwavering commitment to this project.

To all the staff at Interlink—especially John Sobhiea Fiscella, Whitney Sanderson, Jennifer McKenna, and Pamela Fontes-May—for your hard work to get this book off the ground.

To my wonderful husband, partner, designer, problem-solver, and occasional cleanup crew, Julian Ramirez: thank you for your endless support, and for putting your time and your heart into this book. You are my immigrant hero.

And finally, a special thank you to my son, the product of so many joined cultures, who makes me want to make the world a better place.